The Art of Book Marketing

Increase your book sales by 700% in 7 days

Harshajyoti Das

VOL 1

Dedication

To my author friends

About the Author

Harshajyoti Das

Harsh is the CEO and Co-Founder of Munmi IT Solutions LLP.

He is a traveler, writer, inbound marketer, entrepreneur and business adviser.

His other books, *How to write content that converts 600% More* and *No SEO Forever* are both bestsellers. He has published over 7 books and is writing his eighth.

He is also the founder of FireYourMentor.com, a platform for self-published authors.

LET'S CONNECT !

I offer all my new releases for FREE or $0.99 to all my readers during launch day. To get notified about the launch, sign up to my mailing list.

Do sign up as a fan here: https://book-marketing.org

(I hate spam as much as you do).

Contact Info:

- **Fan Email:** author@harsh.im
- **Interview/guestposting/Press requests:** press@harsh.im
- **Amazon Author Profile:** http://www.amazon.com/author/harshajyotidas
- **Twitter:** http://twitter.com/jr_sci
- **Facebook:** https://www.facebook.com/harshajyotidas.author
- **LinkedIn:** http://in.linkedin.com/pub/harshajyoti-das/17/28b/52
- **Google+:** https://plus.google.com/+HarshajyotiDas

Author Website: Harsh.Im

CEO at Munmi IT Solutions LLP: Munmi.org

Founder of: FireYourMentor.com

MAILING LIST: https://book-marketing.org

Table of Contents

INTRODUCTION

Six Principles of Persuasion

Set Up Your Weapons Arsenal

My Personal Secret Weapon -- FREE!

Become a Blog Commenting Superstar

Embrace Opportunities

Go Direct

Pre-Launch Marketing

Post-Launch Marketing

Let's Learn From 'The Guy' Himself

Until Next Time . . .

A Note to My Readers

FREE ABM WORKBOOK

My books are more interactive. The *Art Of Book Marketing Workbook* is a special bonus for my dear readers. It will help you to not just learn the facts but also implement them. Please use the workbook after finishing each chapter to revise what you have learned.

Go to : Book-Marketing.org

INTRODUCTION

I am a self-published author. I have self-published seven books via Amazon and most of my sales used to come without any marketing or promotion. Amazon does most of the selling for me. All I needed to do was to write a good book and put it out there in the market.

I wasn't convinced, since I have been an online marketer for seven years. The fire inside my marketing brain was still burning. I needed to explore the infinite possibilities of promoting a self-published book. The idea of self-publishing is a blessing for many authors and I want to help them accomplish their goals. Thus, the idea to write this book was born.

I will assume that you have already published your book via Amazon, Smashwords, Lulu or one of the other popular self-publishing platforms. I personally publish my digital books on Kindle and Paperbacks via Createspace (both are owned and managed by Amazon). If you still have any query related to self-publishing, send me an email. If you have not self-published for the first time, I would suggest reading the free advice by Aaron on his website, www.newselfpublishing.com.

Let me tell you what you should expect

from this book.

I have very little first-hand experience with physical book marketing. Hence, I have received help from tons of other marketers and publicists to write about offline book marketing. I have worked on my strengths. I have been an online marketer for seven years. I will help you to promote your books online in the most effective way.

Most books already available in the market talk about "where" one can promote instead of "how" one can promote. It's easy to say use Twitter, Facebook, interviews, speaking engagements and get press to sell more books, but nobody talks about how to actually implement them. **The answers we authors seek are "how" not "where."** If you are looking for a "USP" (unique selling proposition) for this book, this is it. I focus on "how" instead of "where."

Online marketing trumps offline marketing since it is cheaper, less time-consuming, and can be automated. The target audience is also easily accessible. Once you set everything up, it takes very little effort to do the promotion.

You won't get a view on how to market a book from a third person's perspective. There are already plenty of articles on the internet that talk about promoting your book via social media, email marketing, etc.

Who am I to give advice on Book Marketing?

I am an author, just as you are. I haven't sold millions of copies (yet), but I have managed to publish seven books in my very first year. I earn enough to live on book royalties alone. I do not have a day job. I am still growing and I want you to be a part of this journey.

This book was not written to give *advice*. I have written this book to *share* what I do to promote my book.

Instead of reading a book written by a "guru," you will be hearing from a fellow author. I hope you will be able to relate better to this since I have gone through the same challenges that you are going through.

I am a lifetime student and try to learn whenever life gives me a chance. I have learned a lot from millionaire authors about book marketing. For the last seven years, I have been in online marketing which has helped me greatly to learn some skills. I have spent countless hours reading books on marketing, psychology, human behavior and listening to interviews. With this book, I have tried to save you the precious hours of going through the same process that I have gone through. You will get a summary of what I know and the "shortcuts" to skip the tedious hours of research and experimenting. You can learn what works and what doesn't work when it comes to online book marketing from my failures.

I have decided to take a whole new approach in writing this book. I will walk you through how I market my books. I have also interviewed numerous authors and will share their secrets to promote books. I have been documenting every step carefully. I will try to be as detailed as possible.

This isn't an endeavor of just one person (me), but hundreds of others. This book wouldn't have been possible with the help of many other authors whom I have been in touch with regularly. They have shared their secrets and helped me produce a book that will help any first time author to promote his/her book.

This book was primarily written for non-fiction writers who target a specific niche/audience; although fiction writers will also be able to gain valuable knowledge.

There's no definite answer to marketing. Marketing itself means innovation. Each and every author will need to work his way up with some unique ideas of his or her own. There are specific triggers in our brain. Whenever we read a good book or listen to a podcast, these triggers are activated. We go through a phase called "conceptual blending," where we mix the ideas of the author/speaker with our old ideas/techniques. We can then come up with a brand new idea that's more refined and unique in its own way.

According to the theory of "conceptual blending," different elements, ideas, techniques and correlations from different scenarios are "blended" in our subconscious mind. This concept will be the basis of coming up with a brand new book marketing strategy while you are reading this book.

Come to think of it, even I have used "conceptual blending" while writing this book. I have taken knowledge from my *seven years of experience as an internet marketer, as well as reading twenty fat books on marketing and self-publishing by various authors, by listening to more than fifty podcasts by top marketers, by watching over fifty videos on marketing, by reading hundreds of articles on book publishing, marketing and psychology, by interviewing hundreds of authors, by spending countless hours on FB groups interacting with self-published authors and by experimenting with hundreds of techniques with my personal books, in order to understand what works and what doesn't.* The ideas from all of these different sources were then blended inside my subconscious mind to finally come up with these easy, simple and unique strategies to promote a book.

Marketing is not a fixed strategy

According to Dan Ariely, author of *Predictably Irrational,* marketing is all about providing information that will heighten someone's anticipation and real pleasure.

A person will buy your product when it matches his expectations. Now, as a smart marketer, your purpose is to exceed his expectations.

Let's say a reader wants to read a book on psychology. Which book do you think will sell better – one that has four chapters in the Table of Contents or one with eighteen chapters?

Take this same example once again. Do you think a book with 45 pages will sell better or a book with 250 pages?

I have published over twenty books using different pen names and I can tell you one thing for sure. Books with more pages and chapters sold ten times more than others. Some might argue that 46 page books are also selling, which I agree with, but these are exceptionally good books. When you take the average of all the two million kindle books on Amazon, you will find that books with more page numbers and chapters sell more.

Book marketing is an amalgamation of simple tips. Nobody can give you a unique strategy to sell hundreds of copies because there is not just one strategy that can sell more books. You will need to tweak your book and techniques a few hundred times in order to see results.

With this book, I have tried my best to show the infinite possibilities for promoting your book. What has worked for me might not work for you, but that doesn't mean that the book is useless. Your goal behind reading this book should be to come up with new ideas on your own.

Just ask yourself: how can you use these techniques in your own unique way? Uniqueness wins every time, because the world is filled with copycats trying to use the same marketing strategies, the same advertising taglines and what not. It is okay to copy success, but you should pour your own uniqueness into the mix.

There are thousands of marketing techniques, but we can't focus on every one of them. It's just not worth our time. Do you remember the Pareto principle of the 80-20 rule, 20% of your effort will produce 80% of the results? We will focus on that 20% effort to give us a competitive edge over our competitors.

There is always a way to do the same thing in a lot of different ways to produce the optimum result. <u>Example:</u> You can personally walk to fifteen different bookstores in your city and request them to store a few copies of your book, or you can email a thousand bookstore owners from across the globe with the same request, but this time, it will only take a minute using automation.

If I were to give just one piece of advice to a new author, it would be to "capture your reader's email," so that you can promote your next book directly to them. Do not rely on an external service like Amazon, Facebook or Twitter to reach your audience. They can change their policy at any time and then you will be left with nothing. Having direct access to your audience should be your ultimate goal.

A lot of bands built their fan base on Myspace, but once Facebook became an industry leader in the social networking industry, these same bands are now struggling to survive. Facebook and Twitter are working today, but are you sure that they will work ten years from now? The only way to secure your future is to build an email list instead of focusing your energy on gaining Twitter followers and Facebook likes. Do not assume followers and likes are your sole audience. Just think of them as your bonus audience.

Always remember that it's easier to keep a present customer than to gain a new one. If a reader has committed to buy one of your books, he will probably buy your second book if he likes your first book.

Direct marketing is your answer to success. You might have heard many people tell you the same thing again and again, but it's true. It might sound like common advice, but you cannot afford to ignore it. You need to capture their emails, if not their phone numbers and home addresses. Email marketing is easier than sending physical mail, right?

Now, let's get started with the book!

Chapter 1

Six Principles of Persuasion

Robert B. Cialdini has written a great book on behavioral marketing called *Influence: The Psychology of Persuasion*. The six principles he talks about in his book are reciprocity, commitment/consistency, social proof, liking, authority and scarcity. We will apply some of these common persuasion techniques to create our marketing strategies.

Let me give you a few examples on how we can use his principles and apply it to book marketing.

Reciprocity

First, think about what you want from the other person. Then, think about what you can offer him so that he feels like it's an obligation to return the favor. Let's say you need some book reviews. If you ask your readers blatantly, you will sound too needy. Instead, think of what you can offer them so that they feel obliged to return a favor. You can offer them some exclusive content, a free consultation, signed copies, autographs, t-shirts, a pen or even a bunch of flowers mailed to their home address.

If you have previously helped someone in the past, you can also remind them of this and ask for a favor this time. Hence, find your target audience and opportunities to help them in any way you can (even when they don't ask for it). A simple way to do so in this digital world is to promote someone else's work. If an author in your niche has written a good book, share it with your fans and followers. Make sure he knows you have done this. When the time comes, you can ask him to do the same and he will feel obliged to return the favor. It's a natural tendency and that's how human beings behave.

I tried something similar with a few randomly hand-picked email subscribers. I sent each one of them an e-greetings card by email for Christmas (I used www.123greetings.com). I made sure that each e-greetings card was personalized and had their name on it. Each one of them wished me back. I immediately asked them to tweet about a free promo I was running during the holidays. I made it easy for them by creating a 1-click tweet link using http://clicktotweet.com. A whopping 73% complied with my request.

Another way of using the rule of reciprocity is by helping other authors in your niche. They will start helping you in return. I will tell you how I am doing it, but before I do, let me share how bloggers are using the same rule to promote themselves with the help of fellow bloggers. We can use the same techniques to promote our book instead of our blog.

Now-a-days, most blogs entertain guest bloggers. Let's say you and I are both bloggers in the parenting niche. I will invite you to write an article in my blog as a guest author. After publishing your article, wouldn't you share it on Twitter and Facebook and possibly even email your subscribers? You are not only sending them to your article, but you are directing them to my blog.

What if I interviewed you on my blog? Wouldn't you share it with your audience? What if I just mentioned you in my blog along with five other people? Wouldn't you share it again with your audience? It's not uncommon to see Facebook page updates like, "Hey, check out my latest interview with XYZ on ABC.com," or "I was mentioned in XYZ blog in an article about ABC. Check it out."

There's another way to do the same thing. Let me tweet your book right now and ask you to tweet mine. Would you do it? Of course you would. You would feel guilty if you don't return the favor. It's natural human tendency. Now, there will be a small percentage of people who will ignore this, but we are not talking about them here. They are the ones who will always turn a blind eye to every opportunity.

Yesterday, I went out to a couple of strangers on Twitter and asked them to promote my interview. I didn't go up to any stranger, only to people who actively tweeted using the hashtag #bookmarketing. Here's how the conversation went:

Harshajyoti Das @jr_sci · Oct 21
Mind if you TWEET my latest interview about Book Marketing?
bkc.name/how-to-hit-ama… CC @DIYauthor @IndiesBookPromo @bkmkting @Nicholas_Rossis

DIY Author @DIYauthor · Oct 22
Podcast: How to hit Amazon Bestseller List without Subscribers with Harshajyoti Das buff.ly/ZGvCyd @jr_sci @BernardKelvin

DIY Author @DIYauthor · Oct 22
@jr_sci @BernardKelvin I have a link to the episode scheduled to go out later today. :)

Harshajyoti Das @jr_sci · 2m
@DIYauthor Sure, send it over and I will tweet it. Thanks for your share. CC @BernardKelvin

In my first screenshot, I asked them to tweet about my book. The second screenshot shows that "DYI Author" sent out a tweet. In the third screenshot, he asked if I was willing to tweet his interview. The reciprocation rule started playing shortly after I saw his message. I couldn't say "no" to him. It was as if I went into an autopilot mode. I immediately told him that I tweeted it.

The rule of reciprocation undeniably works for each and every one of us. Most of the time, it's on an unconscious level. We need to consciously keep looking for opportunities where we can use the rule of reciprocation. If you aren't excited to know about this powerful psychological tool even now, how about I modify my statement?

You can hypnotize a person to do anything you want if you use the 'rule of reciprocation' in a clever way.

Now, it sounds like something, doesn't it?

Commitment/Consistency

When a person commits to a small request, he is much more likely to commit to a bigger request. If you ask a buddy of yours to tweet about your book, he is also more likely to commit to a bigger request, such as buying your book (which will of course cost him money). If you would have asked him to buy the book directly, the acceptance rate would have been much less.

I will give you two different instances to help you understand this concept more clearly.

Instance 1:

You link to the "Amazon Sample" directly from your website, with a link like this: www.amazon.com/dp/ASIN/#reader_ASIN. Replace ASIN with your respective ASIN number. Whenever a visitor clicks on that link, the Amazon sample will open up in a new browser.

Instance 2:

You offer a sample of your book on your website, but it's not free. Readers will have to pay with a tweet. Meaning, they will be able to download your sample only after they share it on social media (use something like www.paywithatweet.com or social locker). After they have unlocked it, they will be able to see the same Amazon Sample Link.

A sample social locker button on your website looks like this:

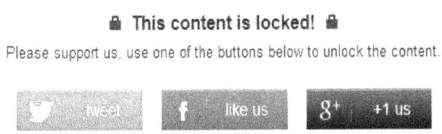

Now which instance do you think will gain more buyers for your book? Obviously the second instance, since that person has already committed to pay "with a tweet." He has a natural tendency to be consistent with his earlier actions. In his mind, if he can "pay" for a sample, then he can definitely "pay" for the whole book (provided he likes the sample).

Obviously, there will be a percentage of people who will not be consistent with their earlier actions. If you go by statistics, the conversion rate on "instance 2" will be more than that of "instance 1" by at least 50%. The conversion rate in this case is to buy your book after reading your sample. It means you will get 50% or more buyers if you implement "instance 2" on your website instead of "instance 1."

This is the main reason why an old reader is your best future reader. Since he has already brought your book, he is more likely to buy your second book.

When you capture their email ID, you have direct access to your audience. You can send them a follow-up email asking if they have purchased your other books. A higher percentage of people will actually buy your book if you merely point them to your other books. It's been tested and proven.

As an author, we do not earn a lot from our books. If we sell our book for $2.99, we earn a royalty of $2 per book. Authors who are outside the U.S. will again have to pay 30% of that amount as tax withholding. That leaves us with $1.40 per book. Again, we are subjected to tax to our local government, which is between 20% and 30%. Ultimately, we only earn about $1.00 per book. We can all complain that it's not justified for all the hard work we put into writing a book, but that's the reality. Hence, most authors also have a day job to help with the financial burden.

It becomes even more important for an author to learn the art of up-sell. There's nothing to be shy of when up-selling a product to your readers. Even authors have the right to live a decent life and for that we need money. Book royalties are not always enough in this economy.

You can up-sell a course, another book or a consultation. "The Law of Commitment & Consistency" comes into play even here. Readers who have previously bought your book will be more likely to buy a course you are selling directly through email.

Capitalize on their buying behavior to make up for the book that you have just sold for a net profit of $1.00.

The idea of Commitment & Consistency goes a long way. If a reader is likely to respond to your email message, he/she is also more likely to post a review. All you need to do is ask for it.

Social Proof

A person is more likely to buy your book if he sees that others are also buying it. Hence, the more the reviews (whether good or bad) that a book has, typically the better it will sell than one with no reviews. You need to make potential readers believe that other people are already reading your book.

If you have a Facebook fan page with very little likes, your readers will be hesitant to "like" your fan page. However, if you have 10,000 likes on your author page, won't it make a solid impact whenever someone visits your fan page? Some readers will make a purchasing decision by seeing your like count alone. You can also leverage your "popularity" by highlighting it within the book or product page. I realize that 10,000 likes will cost you a fortune if you were to try Facebook advertising. So, first figure out how many "likes" you really need. How many likes does an author in your niche typically have? If you target an achievable number, such as 2000 likes, it won't be tough. The first initial likes are only for social proof. You aren't selling them your book. Hence, instead of targeting a specific group of people from the U.S., target a broad audience from Asia. Create an attractive giveaway to get quick likes. Your likes will cost you less (usually around $0.03/like). Going by that calculation, it will cost you just $60 for your initial 2000 likes.

The same goes for Twitter followers. You need to increase your Twitter followers. A few hundred followers won't make a good impression for an author. With Twitter, it's really easy to gain followers. Just follow people and they are going to follow you back. It's as simple as it can get. Use free services like www.justunfollow.com.

For your tweets on Twitter, always use a #hashtag with your book name. It will help you spread the word. Every person who re-tweets your tweets will then have the #hashtag in their tweets and it will ultimately increase your reach.

Do what you have to do to make people think that there are a lot of readers who buy your book. Testimonials, editorial reviews, increased Facebook Fans, Twitter followers, massive comments on each of your blog posts, all of these increase the social share count on your blog posts, etc.

Social proof is not only about gaining new buyers but also to prevent people from following a crowd. If a book receives negative reviews one after the other, then chances are the subsequent reviewer who was planning to leave a positive review will start nitpicking for errors in your book. Instead of leaving a 5 star review, he will leave a 4 star review. In these scenarios, you should be as polite as possible, but contradict their verdicts and break that chain. Contact a couple of loyal email subscribers and request them to write their reviews if they haven't already. Use the reciprocation technique using e-greetings card if you have to. If you don't do that, the chain of negative reviews will go on and on.

Likeability:

I can't tell you how powerful this element is. Whenever you launch a product (say a book) there will be a percentage of people who will buy it no matter what. These groups of people will buy anything you sell.

Well, think of this scenario. Who is your favorite Hollywood actor? Won't you run to the theatres as soon as his new movie releases?

A couple of days ago, I created a $150.00 consulting gig to help authors promote their books. At first, I contacted some friends on Facebook. Almost 70% of the people I contacted immediately bought my gig without asking too many questions. Next, I tried to contact a few old clients with whom I have done business before. Just 10% of them brought my gig this time. Lastly, I tried cold-calling a handful of authors. I have never done any business with them, nor have I done any business before. It was no surprise that only 1% of them brought my service.

The ideal conversion rate when you try to sell a product or a service to an unknown audience is 1% to 2%, but do you see how you can easily raise that figure to a 70% conversion rate just by adding "liking" to the business environment?

How tough is it to get in somebody's good book?

It can be extremely easy for you if you do it right and similarly, it will be extremely hard for you if you do it wrong.

First of all, how do you make someone like you? Not just in business, but in personal life?

It's really easy. Be good to them, help them, greet them, praise them, or in other words, shower them with positive energy.

This reminds me of a chapter I have written in my other book on *How to be a Ball of Positive Energy*. You can read it here:

http://amzn.to/1vHmR50

You need to come across as a genuine person who really cares for the people around him. It's not the secret for getting people to like you, but it's one of the characteristics.

Most of us have already started building an email list. So, what do we email our subscribers? Let me ask this question differently. Do you send only marketing emails? When was the last time you sent an email just greeting them on their birthday or for Christmas?

It really doesn't take much of an effort to get in somebody's good book. Be their friend, be with them when they need you and help them without expecting anything in return. Most of my new readers are my old readers. Do you know why? Because I connect with them on a personal level. The first time they subscribe to my list, I will email and ask them if there's anything I could do to solve a problem they are facing presently. I also make sure to reply to reply to each and every email. It takes a lot of time, but the effort to make a connection is worth it.

Here's an exercise I want you to try:

Imagine one of your previous readers entering a local bookstore with her friend. She sees your book on the shelves. Instead of saying, "Hey look, I read that book by this author," what can you do to make her say, "Hey look, my friend wrote that book." Find a notebook and write down everything you can do to make it happen. The next step is to implement it.

The next question that comes up is, "What if I have hundreds and thousands of readers? How do I possibly reply to each one of their queries?" The honest truth is, you wouldn't be reading this book if you had sold hundreds and thousands of copies. If you have bought this book by mistake, please request a refund. I have written this book for authors who are selling less than 1000 copies per month. Secondly, notice what James Altucher does. He holds a weekly Q&A on Twitter and replies to questions from readers. Now this is a guy who gets over a million visitors to his blog every month. You just need to have the desire to do it.

Authority

What does Authority really mean? Let me explain.

We all are authors here. So, when it comes to writing, whose advice would you blindly take into consideration? It's **Stephen King** - who else?

An authority is a person whose advice we are

likely to accept with our eyes closed, without giving a second thought to his opinion. He is both knowledgeable and a leader in his industry.

I am a big fan of guys like Robert B. Cialdini, Tony Robbins, Dale Carnegie, Derek Halpern, Timothy Ferriss and James Altucher, among others, and 90% of the time, I blindly trust them when they suggest something about business and marketing. That's the power of authority!

How to be an authority?

I was the only kid in my neighborhood who knew how to operate a computer *(in the era of Pentium III),* so my neighbors considered me an authority when it came to computers. If someone had to buy a new laptop, they would come to my house to seek my advice. If someone needed to buy an antivirus program, they would again come to me for my advice. I was just another non-techie kid, but they expected me to fix their computer every time it crashed. They were like, "Harsh knows everything about computers," and I was like, "No, I don't. I just know how to play Road Rash."

Now, take that example and apply it in your business/niche/genre. If you can establish yourself as an authority, people are going to look up to you. They will trust what you have to say and they will buy your book as soon as it is ready for pre-orders. There's no denying that.

I am not an authority (not yet, but maybe I will be after this book). Hence, I can't really tell you how to be an authority, but I can surely share what I am doing in order to become an authority.

First of all, chose a niche. Let's say it's "book marketing" for me.

Secondly, people love consuming new information. So, be the one to pour new information in your niche. Don't say what everybody else is saying. You should be the one to generate fresh ideas.

Thirdly, find a medium to reach your audience. It's perhaps the most important point of all. There are a lot of highly skilled people, but their ideas, their knowledge never reaches the general public. They lack a medium to reach their audience. Thus, it stops them from becoming an authority in their niche. A medium can be anything from a book, blog, social networking, TV or even a YouTube channel.

If people love your ideas, your philosophies, they will accept you as an authority in their niche.

What happens when we are an authority?

Being an authority is not a goal but a continuous journey. Once you establish yourself as an authority in your niche, you will need to maintain that position. There's fierce competition and everybody wants to become an authority in their respective niche.

Keep doing what you have been doing. Just rinse and repeat.

Scarcity

Scarcity is a very powerful tool indeed. A couple of months back, I upgraded my club membership. The sales guy told me that the offer was valid just for the next three days. I immediately took advantage of that offer. I ended up paying $3000.00 for the upgrade, just to save $500.00. I could have lived without making that upgrade. In fact, I was quite happy with my present membership level.

I am sure even you have been a victim of this brilliant marketing technique. We see it everywhere in our day-to-day life. "Just for today," or "Only 2 days left" are common practices among marketers. So, what's stopping authors from taking advantage of this strategy?

But the big question is, **how**?

You can price your book at 99 cents for a limited

period of time. Contact a few people you know and ask them to help you promote it to their audience. You can also update it in your description as "99 cents for the next 100 copies" or something similar.

When someone purchases your first book, you can even give your second book for FREE for a very limited period of time. I will talk about the power of FREE later in the book.

You can combine FREE with SCARCITY to create a unique combination and powerful marketing strategy. When you offer something for free, people will go crazy over it, just so they can grab your offer. It works even better when you offer something for free just for one day. You will grab more attention and interest.

Here's the biggest kept secret:

Whenever you promote a book to an audience put a deadline or a limit if you want people to take action.

E.g.:

- My Kindle book is available at 99 cents only for today.
- Buy a paperback and get the Kindle version for free (valid until tomorrow).
- I am giving away ten signed copies of my

book via this contest.
- Ten lucky Webinar attendees will receive a copy of my book.
- Buy two of my books and get my third book for free (valid only till next Monday).

There are a number of ways you can come up with new offers and promotions. When you have a new offer every month, people will find it more interesting than if you were to run the same offer for a whole year.

Make sure to attach scarcity to that offer. When you tell them that the offer is limited, it prevents procrastination.

People feel threatened when somebody tries to take away their freedom. When you put a limit or a deadline on something, you take away their freedom to buy that product at their will. If the stock doesn't last, they will never be able to avail themselves of that offer. Thus, they act as soon as they can to preserve their freedom to buy that product.

Chapter 2

Set Up Your Weapons Arsenal

1. Facebook author page
2. Twitter profile
3. Book website
4. Personal author website - press kit
5. Public/personal/press emails
6. Pinterest profile
7. Aweber profile
8. HARO/Quora account
9. Google Alerts

Facebook Author Page

Every well-known author has a Facebook page. You can interact directly with your readers or post an update about your new book without sounding like a salesman. Unlike Twitter, you can post pictures and videos as well. Setting up a Facebook author profile is easy. It takes just a few clicks and you are done.

The best feature is probably the custom "giveaway tab" that will help you gain likes by hosting giveaways from time to time. You will need to install the free app.

While we are discussing Facebook author pages, here is my page: https://www.facebook.com/harshajyotidas.author. LIKE it to stay in touch with me directly.

There are a number of ways to earn Facebook likes (oh no, not another list)!

1. Ask readers inside the book to like your Facebook page.
2. Run Facebook ads to get new likes.
3. Have an email signature with a link to your Facebook page.
4. Ask your email subscribers to like your fan page.
5. Link Twitter with Facebook and set up an automated direct message on Twitter (using software such as Tweetadder).
6. Ask your friends and family to like and share your page/posts.
7. Join online groups and communities and promote your Facebook fan page.

Twitter
Twitter is easy to use and people love it. Personally, I love using Twitter because it saves me the time of writing a 300 word email. I need to reduce myself to just 140 characters. Hats off

to the founders of Twitter who came up with this idea.

Twitter makes it extremely simple for people to follow you. It's not necessary that you follow them back. An author cannot follow each and every reader. Hence, Twitter makes a perfect social networking site where readers can follow their favorite author.

To earn the first set of followers, you will need to follow others. Twitter has an unwritten code of conduct that says, "I will follow you back if you follow me."

Also remember to pin a tweet that takes the reader directly to the landing page for your book. Check out how I do it (don't forget to follow): https://twitter.com/jr_sci

I have a book on social media marketing called, *Engagement Interaction Conversion* (http://amzn.to/1sWn9yB). You can read it to get a detailed idea on how you can leverage the power of social media.

I will cut myself short here and won't go into detail on how to use Twitter, as this book is primarily focused on book marketing. If you know how to leverage social media networks like Facebook and Twitter, then you can sell any product, whether it's a book or a weight loss pill.

Let me jump right to the next element, "A book website."

Book Website

This gets interesting here. When I say book website, I don't really mean a website. I mean just a domain name. You needn't build a website around it.

You need to redirect your website to your Amazon's book product page.

Our main idea behind creating a book page is to have a link that can be shared and remembered easily. Still not getting it? Alright, answer this: Which of these two links are easy to remember?

1. Book-marketing.org
2. http://www.amazon.com/Art-Book-Marketing-Increase-PROMOTION-ebook/dp/B00NUKB1Y6/

Without a doubt, it's the first link. It's plain and simple. You can easily share it with your audience on social media, email it or even link it in a press release, guest article, etc.

There's little difference on how the website looks like before and after the release of the book.

Before the release: Redirect the website to a landing page to capture email address of potential readers.

After the release: Redirect the website to your Amazon's book page.

What do I recommend for a landing page?

I use the free theme for Wordpress called "Launch effect." Some people prefer Leadpages and Unbounce.

How do you redirect your domain?

It's absolutely easy.

Option 1: Just go to cpanel, select the redirect option.
Option 2: Redirect using htaccess file.
(Here's a guide http://moz.com/learn/seo/redirection)
Option 3: Install Wordpress on the domain and use a plugin called, "Simple 301 Redirects."

Personal Author Website

A personal author's website is the ultimate destination for anyone who wants to learn about an author, as it will have all of the contact details, author bio, link to his/her books and book burbs.

Check out my site to get a quick idea on what an author page should look like: www.harsh.im

I have seen authors with what they call a website on a free domain like xyz.blogspot.com. Honestly, it's a big turn-off. Not only does it look ugly, but it also looks completely unprofessional. If an author can't buy a domain worth $10.00, what makes you think he is serious about his craft? Now, some people will justify blogspot.com as being easy, but hey, have you used Wordpress? It's even easier than blogpost.com.

Some people also call it the press kit. If media personal wants to interview you tomorrow, this is the place where he will find all the information about you.

Why am I talking about having a website in a book about book marketing? Well, because it's directly related. How will you promote your book if you don't even have the basics right? This is book marketing. Book marketing is not just a campaign on how to sell books overnight. It's the overall process that contains elements such as creating a press kit.

Here are a few things you need to include in your website:

1. Create a one page scroll website instead of many tabs (check www.Harsh.im).
2. Fan email, press email.
3. Author bio (short and full).
4. Author photos.
5. List of books and links.
6. Link to all social media networks.
7. Book blurbs, reviews.
8. Past interviews, guest posts, web mentions.
9. Sample interview questions.
10. Sample tweets/social posts for your fans to promote your book.
11. Sample banners for your brand/books.

Stop procrastinating. It doesn't cost thousands of dollars to create a website. It doesn't even cost $50.00.

Here are your options (seriously! Why again?):

Option 1 *(Total cost: $50.00 + Hosting fees)*: Get a Wordpress theme from Themeforest worth $50.00 and install it on your Wordpress blog. Host it with any major company. Go for godaddy or bluehost.

Option 2 *(Total cost: $49.00)*: My company, Munmi IT Solutions, LLP will take care of your website, hosting, themes, installation and everything for a meager $49.00 per year. Just get in touch with the technical team at support@munmi.org. Tell them that you have purchased this book and that you want to set up an author website.

What kind of domain name is preferable?

Get a domain name that can be remembered easily. If you have a long name like me, get a shorter version of the name. Again, it doesn't matter whether you get a .com or a .me. As long as it's unique, short and brandable, it's good.

I would recommend going for a domain name like, john.com/me/im/net/org. If your first name is not available, get a combination of your first name and last name like Johndoe.com. You can also add "author" after your first name and get a domain such as Johnauthor.com. Since most of the top-level domain names are already taken (.com, .net, .org), I prefer .me and .im domains. They sound great for a personalized author website.

Public/personal/press emails

It might not make sense right now, but you need to get separate email addresses for yourself.

Here are a few examples:

author@domain.com
press@domain.com
contact@domain.com
fan@domain.com
yourname@domain.com
bookname@domain.com

Once you have separate email addresses, it will help you segregate and prioritize which email you want to check. You might want to check your press@domain.com every day, but your fan@domain.com email just 2 or 3 times in a week.

It also gives you the option to have different email signatures for each email ID. For fan@domain.com, you can have an email signature that says, "Please review my book," and your press@domain.com email can have a signature with links to your social media profiles.

Pinterest profile

I keep talking about the undiscovered powerhouse of traffic, "Pinterest," whenever I get a chance.

Create a Pinterest profile if you don't have it already and start a couple of boards on various topics related to your book. Then all you have to do is "**PIN.**" Pin about 100 images every day. Link each image to your landing page and capture their emails. You can also send them to your amazon page, but there's little chance that they will convert. Pinterest visitors are in the surfing mode, not in the buying mode. Hence, it makes more sense to send them to a landing page where they can download the first 3 chapters of your book for free.

From what I have seen, if you pin 100 images daily for a month, you can have a continuous stream of 20 to 30 daily visitors after that, with no work. Pinterest is highly viral. Once you set up everything, the pins keep getting re-pinned from other members, thus increasing your chance to reach a wide audience.

I know it can be tiring to do it manually, so I recommend using software. (http://fireyourmentor.com/pinblaster-review)

If you want to read more about how to engage and convert using Pinterest, read my other book, *Engagement Interaction Conversion* (http://amzn.to/1sWn9yB).

Aweber profile

Most people prefer Mailchimp because it's free until you exceed 2000 subscribers, but I prefer Aweber because it has much more functionality than Mailchimp. With Mailchimp, it will actually cost you the same as Aweber once you exceed 2000 subscribers. Do you want to limit yourself to just 2000 subscribers for the rest of your life?

Aweber forms are better than Mailchimp forms. They are easy to integrate into any landing page via Javascript or you can even let Aweber host them for you.

Most third-party software accepts Aweber's API to easily export your list. (Example: leadpages, unbounce, launcheffect, etc).

It costs $19.00 per month, but if you are serious about your career as an author, this is a small investment. Most people claim that their email subscribers are worth $3.00 to $5.00. This means they earn an average of $3.00 to $5.00 from each of their email subscribers.

If I have 500 subscribers and I promote a course worth $20.00 to my email list, I just need one person to sign up to break even. If I can get 50 people to sign up, I will earn $1000.00. If you take the average, each subscriber will then be worth $2.00. It's a number game.

If not Aweber, you can also sign up to Getresponse or Mailchimp. It's completely up to you.

HARO Account:

HARO stands for "help a reporter out." It's a site where reporters come looking for a source for their queries. If you have enough knowledge about a particular query, you can answer directly and you might just get a chance to be featured in a national newspaper.

I have to agree, however, that the market is super competitive. A reporter gets anywhere from 20 to 100 queries within 1 to 2 hours from a lot of sources. Your answer should stand out in order to qualify.

I used HARO to get mentioned here:

- http://blog.mycorporation.com/2014/05/experts-weigh-im-twentysomething-entrepreneur/
- http://new-talent-times.softwareadvice.com/morale-boosters-gone-wrong-0714/

I don't use it as a prime marketing tool. I will tell you about that in a bit. The hard work you put into answering each and every query is not worth the result. There's a 1% to 2% chance that you will be picked. In other words, you will have to answer to 50 to 100 queries and only one or two might be accepted. Each answer will have to be about 200 to 300 words. You will end up writing 20,000 to 30,000 words (the equivalent of a book) in the whole process. Is it worth it? Not for me, but you might give it a try.

Some authors can also hire qualified VA's to do the job for them.

What's an alternative? (Now that's more like it . . .)

Of course, there are other alternatives like Quora. It's a Q&A site just like "Yahoo Answers." Many reporters look to Quora to find their source.

Here's how Quora stands out. When you post a reply to a query on Quora, the answer is posted publicly. If you post a link back to your author website/book, you can expect some traffic as well. Now, not all queries posted on Quora are by journalists. The majority of the queries are posted by people like you and me, but if you ask me, it's worth the hard work when you compare it with HARO.

I need something better than HARO and QUORA!

Don't worry, I've got you covered. The answer is "Blog commenting."

I recently published a book called, _Zero Advertising Cost, Blog Commenting Rocks_. I have also invited Ryan Biddulph, author of *Blogging from Paradise*, to do an interview (you will find it later in this book) on how he leveraged blog commenting to get mentioned in over 50 sites within a month.

Imagine if you were given an opportunity to publish on Forbes. Would you grab it? Of course you would. What people don't realize is that the opportunity still exists. In fact, it's FREE!

You can post a blog comment on almost any major website. Don't just write feedback for that article, but post a big fat comment that looks like a mini blog post. It will add value to the original article. You will get noticed by the author and the staff members. Once they know that you are an authority in your niche, they will approach you for an interview and even call you to write a guest article. You will build new relationships with people of authority in your industry. The possibilities are endless.

Blog commenting works better than anything else because it allows you to connect directly with an influential person. When you post a blog post, don't you get excited to read the comments? You will be even more excited when that comment is not a one liner like "cool post," but a 300 word in-depth comment that adds value to your blog post. What if that person comes back each and every time you post a blog post? Don't you think it will create a bond between the two of you? Think of the whole scenario as the content creator. You will understand how powerful blog commenting can be from the perspective of an author trying to get noticed.

I will keep it short for now. I have a chapter on blog commenting, but I highly advise you to grab my book, *Zero Advertising Cost, Blog Commenting Rocks*, so that you can get into detail about this massive source of traffic.

Let's move on to our next element, "Google Alerts."

Google Alerts

When you set up "Google Alerts," you will be able to receive an email whenever a new search result appears.

Let's say you set up an alert for "Your Name." Whenever someone talks about you, you will receive an email with the site link. It's an amazing tool for staying connected with your audience.

However, there are also some other innovative ways to use "Google Alerts."

- You can set up an alert for the name of another author or his book
- You can set up alerts for "keywords" relative to your genre/niche

Let's talk about setting up alerts for another author's name and book. Whenever a site mentions him, you can go to that site and see if there's a way to leave a blog comment.

The main idea behind this strategy is to make yourself visible. The site owner who has written about the other author will see your comment. If you keep trying this strategy again and again, ultimately you will be known and chances are that you will be invited by these blog owners to do an interview or write a guest post.

Eighty percent of success is showing up. - **Woody Allen**

You are not only building a long term strategy, but there are some short term benefits as well. Visitors who read about the other author will also see you. That's how you can attract new readers to read your book, because they are already used to reading similar books.

Chapter 3

My Personal Secret Weapon -- FREE!

The word FREE has a distinct effect on all of us. It also affects our judgment when it comes to buying. Most often, we end up buying things we don't need.

Let's say you go to a shopping mall to buy a nice pair of jeans. When you visit the store, you see that they have a "buy 2, get 1 free" offer. We quickly fall prey to such an offer. Even when we don't need three pairs of jeans, we will pay more because we are getting a pair for free.

Marketers have been cashing in on the concept of FREE for generations. If you can master the concept of "FREE," imaging that you will be able to sell almost anything. You can even sell a book that a person wasn't even planning to buy in the first place.

Don't offer discounts. Offer free items.

Let's take the above example. You see two offers when you visit a store.

First offer: Buy 2, get 1 free
Second offer: Buy 3 at a 35% discount

You will choose the first option, right? But did you know that if you would have selected the second offer, you could have saved 2.5% more? That's the power of FREE. It makes us blind. We make an instant decision to grab anything that's free.

With this book, I am giving out ***ABM WORKBOOK*** completely free to my readers. You can grab it here: Book-Marketing.org . I could have sold it for $2.99 as an upsell but then I decided to give it away for free.

If you are enrolled in the KDP select program, you have two options. Either you can give your books away for free or you can run a Kindle countdown for 99 cents. It's a dilemma for most people. Now that you know the power of free, it will be easy for you to make a decision.

Evernote CEO Phil Libin says, "The easiest way to get 1 million people paying is to get 1 billion people using."

My personal advice for any author is to find new avenues to reach more and more readers. Do not worry about earning more money right now. Get some visibility first then think about profit.

A lot of new authors who do not have an audience will price their brand new books for $6.99. My question to them is: do you want to earn more money or earn more readers?

If you price your book at 99 cents you will be able to get more readers and build an audience. Once you do, you can launch your next book and price it at $6.99. If you are able to make one of your books "permanently free" on Amazon, then it's even better.

Create a sales funnel

Asking strangers to buy your book is not the best advice. There are thousands of authors who cry because they cannot get more sales. One of the simple answers to their agony is that they do not have a sales funnel.

Writing a book and publishing it is not enough. You need to have a sales funnel. **You need to treat your book as a business and your readers as clients.**

<u>Here's an example of how to create a sales funnel, taken from a YouTube Video:</u>

If you create a YouTube channel, you will get free visitors organically from the world's second biggest search engine (which is YouTube).

Continue creating a few videos and earn a few hundred subscribers. YouTube videos are free and thus your videos will generate enormous traffic (even without any promotion). Then, launch a "Mega Video," which will have more content and premium information than the other videos. You can talk about your book at the end of this video. Here's what the funnel looks like:

50 Free videos ---> One hundred subscribers ---> One Premium Video ---> Offer book as a free gift---> Earn reviews ---> Earn social shares ---> Sell more books on Amazon

You can create a similar funnel for Slideshare presentations:

Slideshare presentations ---> Capture email address ---> Offer Free book ---> Upsell paid books ---> Upsell paid courses

You can go about creating a sales funnel with almost any medium. It even works in offline marketing.

Lecture in a local school ---> Offer a free book to the school library ---> Students will read your first book ---> They will buy your second book ---> Upsell online courses

You will notice something similar in all of the

above examples. We have offered something for FREE before selling anything. Whether it's a YouTube video, a Slideshare presentation or a lecture in your local school, first you offer your services for free and later you will get the same people to buy from you. This model works perfectly in the modern world.

Most authors do not struggle with money but to get readers

Amazon doesn't give you details about your readers. It's anonymous. The only way you can connect with your readers is by capturing their email addresses. Of course, you can ask them to like you on Facebook or to follow you on Twitter, but in reality, social reach is less 5%.

When you Tweet something or post on your Facebook page, only 20% of people will actually see it and less than 5% will engage with it.

The best way to reach the maximum amount of people is by going direct via email to their inbox.

I will tell you a cost effective way to capture emails using the power of FREE!

As I have previously discussed, email subscribers are worth $3.00 to $5.00, so it makes sense to spend about $1.00 to earn them. In fact, there's a way to earn an email subscriber for just 30 cents.

Offer a FREE $1 Amazon gift card to each and every reader. Tell them that it's a return gift from your side, as a courtesy to say "thank you" for buying your book.

If you are not ready to spend $1.00 for each reader, here's what you can do. Increase your book price by $1.00. If you were previously selling your book for $2.99, price it at $3.99.

Amazon will pay you 70 cents for that extra dollar. Thus, you will earn their emails for just 30 cents.

You can make this idea even more innovative. You can offer a $2.00 gift card in exchange for their email address. Ultimately, it comes down to how much you are willing to spend to earn their email address.

The power of FREE goes a long way. When you give away an assured gift card to each and every reader, only a handful will ignore the offer. Is it against Amazon's TOS? Not at all. It's just clever marketing.

Imagine what you can do after you have captured their email address. You can upsell them your other books, or even a course priced at hundreds of dollars. And most of all, emails are an asset.

Do not confuse social norms with market norms. Paying money to your readers to do a certain task like sharing your book on social media doesn't end well.

Create value out of thin air and offer it as FREE!

Sounds exciting, doesn't it? You can create a free goodie such as entry to a premium giveaway of your signed book, free access to your private forums, free access to your private Facebook group or even a free pass to one of your events.

Offer these free goodies to encourage readers to share your books on social media, post a picture of them holding a book or invite friends to join your Facebook group. You are substituting money with a free goodie. I will explain to you why offering free goodies works better than offering money.

Let's think of a hypothetical situation. You have your daughter's first stage performance tomorrow and you need someone to cover for you in the office. You call one of your colleagues and explain your situation to him. He will happily agree to help you out.

Now imagine if you called him and said, "Matt,

can you cover for me tomorrow? I will pay you $50.00?" It's most likely going to offend him. Even if he agrees for the first time, the next time you ask him for a similar favor, he is most likely to ask, "How much are you going to pay me this time?"

If you really wanted to say thanks, you could have gifted him a bottle of champagne the next day. Gifts do not create obligations or bring the traditional market norms into the picture.

If you pay off your readers to get them to promote the book for you, it's going to backfire. Offer them gifts for their help. Now, gifts can be pretty expensive, hence you can create free goodies out of thin air and offer them as gifts. The possibilities are endless. You just need to sit down and think hard about what you can offer.

When a reader buys your book, he/she is not obliged to leave a review. He pays to read the book, not to help you promote your book. There's no unspoken code of conduct. It purely relies on the market rules, "I will pay you, you give me the product" (Here, the product refers to your book).

It's our duty as smart marketers to shift the market norms to social norms. **In other words, we will need to "turn our readers into fans."**

Don't forget the rule of reciprocation. Offering them free gifts will also make them feel obliged to return the favor. The next time you ask them to tweet about your new release or write a review on Goodreads, they will be happy to oblige.

Chapter 4

Become a Blog Commenting Superstar

For an author, it's extremely hard to get into the nitty gritty of marketing and promotion. Most often, we feel that our job is to write a good book, why should we worry about marketing?

For those who think this way, I have to say something. Treat your books as a business and your readers as customers. The moment you stop promoting your business it will die (unless and until it's a big brand). The same is the case with authors. If you stop promoting your book, there's no way you can expect it to sell well.

Compare yourself with a business owner. Even they have to spend countless hours developing a unique product idea. Then they go through the rigorous task of polishing their product before launching it. Once launched, their next job is to promote it and earn customers. Ultimately, they have to offer customer service to make sure that they have repeated customers.

An author goes through a similar phase. If an

author stops after writing a book and ignores the rest of the process, do you think he can be successful? Either hire a marketing agency or do it yourself, but the bottom line is that you will have to work hard on promotion to get the word out there.

In this chapter, I will talk about one of the free promotional tools that won't cost you any money. It will cost you some time (around 1-2 hours per day).

First of all, you need to have a goal. Don't go about creating a list of short-term and long-term goals now. You need to have just one goal. **The goal is to be seen everywhere.**

Once you make up your mind that you need to be seen everywhere, the rest becomes easy. All you need is a plan to work out a strategy.

First of all, make a list of all the major blogs in your niche. If you are the author of a parenting guide book, find high-traffic blogs that are devoted to parenting. Subscribe to their mailing list using a separate email ID just for this purpose. You don't want to get spammed to death. Whenever you receive a new blog post to your email, all you need to do is visit that blog and post your comment after reading the article.

If you are a fiction writer, it might be a bit of a

challenge for you. Still, do not lose hope. You can follow blogs of famous authors in your niche. It's obvious that their blog will attract a lot of their book readers. When you start commenting on their latest blog posts, you will get noticed. Well, that's our main goal isn't it?

What's the best way to get noticed via blog commenting? Guess!

It's by leveraging the popularity and fan following of a famous author.

Start following blogs that regularly publish podcasts and interviews of authors. Let's say you are a romance book writer. Whenever an interview of another romance writer is published, jump right into listening/reading the interview and post your comment.

As an author, we find great pride in telling the whole world about our interview. We will share it on Facebook and Twitter and will also email our subscribers saying, "My interview was published on XYZ. Go and check it out."

You can leverage the same excitement to get noticed. Their fans and followers will see you and your comment whenever they visit to check out the interview of their favorite author.

No, you don't need to get sales right at that very

moment. That's not our main agenda. With time, you will increase your visibility and more and more people will come to know you by your name and avatar.

When this same audience surfs through Amazon to read a book, they will immediately recognize your name when they see your book. Amazon already does a great job of promoting your book under multiple categories. The only thing that stops the majority of readers from buying our books is that they don't know us personally.

Marketing is a process, not an event.

What's all the buzz about BuzzSumo?

BuzzSumo is like Google, but instead of showing just random pages, it will show you sites that have the maximum social visibility. You will be able to analyze content and find influencers in your industry based on Facebook shares, Twitter shares, LinkedIn shares, Pinterest shares, Google shares, etc.

Let's say you want to find an interview of a romance author that has received maximum social shares. Just type in "Romance Author" and filter by "interview." Similarly, you can also filter the results by "guest post," "infographics," "article," "giveaways" and "videos."

There's another interesting feature in BuzzSumo. You can also find all the people who have shared a particular article. It doesn't end there. You can sort these people based on their engagement, authority, followers and reply ratio.

I know you must be going, "Wow! Why haven't I found out about this tool before?" But wait, I am not done yet. There's more to it.

You can also filter these people based on journalists, influencers, bloggers, companies and normal people. Thus, if you want to contact only bloggers who have shared a particular interview, you can easily do so with a few clicks.

By now, you are probably wondering how you can use it to promote your book. Let's take a hypothetical situation.

You have recently published an interview on an internet radio channel. You want to promote it to an audience. You have shared it with your Twitter followers, but have probably received only three re-tweets. You need more exposure. Here's what you do.

Find the most shared content of that internet radio channel, and type in the website on BuzzSumo. It will analyze all of the interviews published to the current date and will list them based on the most popular content. Find people who have shared the most popular content. Start following them one by one. Wait a day or two, and 30% to 70% should follow you back. Send them a tweet such as:

Hi, {firstname} What's your book? Let me tweet about it. Could you please RETWEET my interview? http://linkurssssl.com @username #interview

It's that simple. Simply ask them to retweet and it takes them a second to hit the retweet button. You are offering to do them a favor and they will automatically feel obliged to return a favor (remember the rule of reciprocity)?

To find new interview opportunities:

You can search for "Bestselling author" and filter the results by "interviews."

The next thing is to create a strategy to get interviewed on that site.

Typical approach: Open the interview, find the contact page and send an email asking for an interview. It works sometimes, but most of the time, your email will be ignored.

The Art of Marketing approach:

1. Open the interview.

2. Post a blog comment on the article.
3. Find the opt-in form and subscribe to the blog.
4. Find the Twitter ID of the blog owner and start following him.
5. Add his Twitter ID to TweetAdder to automatically retweet random tweets.
6. Like his Facebook page. Like and comment whenever he posts an update.
7. Comment on his latest blog posts continuously for a week.
8. Add him to LinkedIn after he has gotten to know you.
9. Contact the blog owner to see if there's an interview opportunity.
10. Wait for four to five days and follow up on your previous email.

Most people do not follow "The Art of Marketing Approach" and hence they end up hitting a dead end.

While we are having this discussion, let me also write a sample email that you can send to a blog owner.

Hello {First name},
I have been following your blog {Blog Name} for quite some time now. I read your interview with {other author's name} and I absolutely

loved it.

I am an author of {Your Book Name}. I was hoping to get interviewed and connect with your blog audience. Are you looking for one?

I wish you all the best in whatever you are doing. If you need any help from me, do not hesitate to ask.

*Regards,
{Your name}*

Author, {your book name}

*www.AuthorWebsite.im
Twitter: @username*

Keep your email short and to the point. Most people check their emails on their phones and they do not have more than 30 seconds to read your email.

I would like to point out that you shouldn't stop interacting with their audience after you have sent out that email. Continue to engage, interact and share their content. If they are not looking for an interviewee right now, they will surely contact you in the future.

Leave meaningful comments

It won't do any good if you use comments just to post your feedback about an article. You need to write something that might help other readers to gain some knowledge. In other words, write an extension of the original article. Write something that the author might have missed. Do your research before writing. If you can link your comments to credible sources, it will validate them.

There's nothing called half-effort or full-effort. If you are doing something, give it your best. How you do anything is how you do everything.

The same applies for blog commenting. If you are writing a comment, make sure you give it your full effort so that it makes an impact on a reader.

A one-liner like, "Good post, thank you for writing this article" will not do you or anybody else any good.

Scratch my back, I'll scratch yours

The "reciprocation rule" applies here as well. When you post a comment on a blog, you are contributing to somebody else's blog. You are adding value to his blog.

Whenever we post something on our blog, YouTube channel, Twitter or on Facebook we keep waiting for that first "comment" or "like." It's a natural human tendency to expect the reward for our hard work.

A comment, share, tweet or a like comes down to us as a reward for our work. We get excited when somebody likes our FB post. We feel the same excitement when someone comments or appreciates our work.

Take the example of book reviews. Don't you feel excited when you receive a new review for your book?

What a review is to a book, a comment is to a blog.

It's an amazingly simple way to build connections. When you post comments on another author's blog regularly, he will recognize you. If he is a very successful author, he can do a lot to help you promote your book to his audience.

Once you have built a relationship, try asking for a simple retweet. There's very little chance that the other person won't comply.

Many bloggers are using blog commenting to leverage traffic to their site. They help each other to send traffic and engagement. If authors combine and form a similar community imagine the readers we can reach.

If you know a couple of guys in your industry, form a small Facebook group. Like and share each other's posts and comment on each other's blogs.

If there are ten members in a small group and each one of them have 5000 followers on Social media, every one of them can reach 50,000 readers and grow as a community.

There's an unspoken rule in blog commenting. You scratch my back, I'll scratch yours. For instance, forget about blog commenting. You must be familiar with commenting on Facebook. Try noticing the trend. People whose posts you like and leave comments for are also more likely to comment and like your posts. **My point is, leverage this strategy to reach more readers and sell more books.**

Use a unique gravatar and name

In a crowded place, it becomes essential that you have a unique identity. Wordpress is the world's most popular blogging platform. Almost every other blog you find on the internet is built on the Wordpress platform.

Wordpress uses gravatars. It's a globally recognized avatar (profile picture) linked to your email address. You can set up a gravatar on http://gravatar.com. Once you are done, you are ready to start your blog commenting journey. Go to any Wordpress site and post a comment using your unique email address. It will automatically pull your profile picture from gravatar.com.

I would also recommend that you use the same gravatar as your profile picture on social media profiles. It helps your audience to identify and easily recognize you. Use your full name while writing a comment. Our whole idea is to brand ourselves. The next time someone surfs through Amazon and sees our name, they should instantly recognize us.

Link back to your blog posts:

Every blog has a space to insert your website. If you have a blog, insert your blog URL. If you don't have a blog, insert the URL of your author's website.

Having a blog has its own advantages. It acts as a source to drive traffic to your site. You can also expect to receive some comments from the same people whose blogs you have left a comment. The rule of reciprocity will start playing its magic.

I don't have a blog. Hence, I prefer linking back to my author website www.harsh.im.

Reply to each and every comment

If you want to build a connection with a large audience, this is the perfect way to do it. Find any article with a lot of comments. You will see that almost every comment will have a query or a statement. You can start replying to each and every comment.

You will not only be the "star commenter" of that article, but you will also get in the limelight. It's another way to brand yourself. People to whom you have replied will start knowing you by your name. The site owner will also recognize you as an authority because he is ultimately the one who will approve all your comments from the Wordpress backend.

You can start following this technique with a few major blogs with a lot of traffic in your niche. First, you will find a lot of similar faces while commenting. Secondly, these articles will attract a lot of traffic. When you reply to twenty comments in any particular article, you will attract eyeballs. It's obvious. This is the beginning of branding yourself. People will start knowing you by your face and name.

Visit your reader's blog and leave a comment. Make them your fan.

You can easily find a reader's blog when they start following you on Twitter or when they email you. Make it a habit of commenting at least once on their blog. This strengthens the bond and they will be your fan forever.

What you have just done is taken a market norm (exchange of money to buy the book) to a social norm (mutual following, commenting). The next time you ask them to leave a review for your book they will more than likely comply.

This goes a long way. As I always say, your best future readers are your present readers. These are the ones who will buy your books again and again. They will also be responsible for sharing your work with the world. If you want to get social shares, you will have to count on your old readers.

When you convert them from "just readers" to "your fans," you are creating an army of supporters.

I had the opportunity to interview Ryan Biddulph, author of *Blogging from Paradise.* This is the guy you should be listening to if you want advice on marketing and branding using blog commenting.

Let's dig into a conversational mode . . .

1. **What's your number one marketing strategy to promote your books? Why?**

I enjoy promoting other eBook authors and bloggers. Doing so earns me karmic brownie points. If you help people, you will be helped. It's that simple. Give whatever you want. I also enjoy giving out a few free copies of my eBooks here and there to spread the word, to gain endorsements and to give my eBooks a bit of a promotional blitz. Giving freely is the way to promote whatever you wish to promote.

2. **How can an author leverage the power of blog commenting to promote his book without sounding like a salesperson?**

Blog commenting is my favorite way to meet new folks, to strengthen bonds and to promote my blog and eBooks. The key is to create value where you show up. I may share my thoughts on the topic being discussed, thanking the blogger for sharing their insight. Then, here and there - not in every comment of course - I may note an eBook, IF the eBook is relevant to the topic being discussed. Take blog commenting, for instance. If a post shares tips for driving traffic through blog commenting, I may note one of my Blogging from Paradise eBooks covers, how to build your online business through commenting. But subtlety counts, so I'll note this in passing, after creating three thorough paragraphs chatting about the post.

3. How frequently do you recommend that an author should comment? How long does it take to see results?

Daily, Harsh. Comment on at least 10 blogs daily. Don't get caught up in the numbers though; each impact you make counts the most. Authors should post three to four paragraph in-depth, thorough comments on relevant authority blogs. If you're a busy 9-5 person who has little time on a set day, just comment on one or two blogs, but make the comments count! Go in-depth, share your wisdom and treat comments like content. Write a mini guest post to make an impact, and to get noticed.

4. Can you share some statistics about your book sales, if you are comfortable with doing so? How many of these sales were directly or indirectly a result of blog commenting?

I do zero metrics for my eBooks. I go only off of feel and intuition. This detaches me from the outcomes, and also has helped me gain two endorsements from a New York Times best-selling author. I have spoken at the prestigious, world renowned university, NYU, in December and this opportunity was presented to me through blog commenting. So, by not focusing on traffic or metrics in terms of my commenting strategy, I received two eBook endorsements from a New York Times bestselling author (who is a business advisor for Richard Branson, Google, Tony Robbins, Microsoft, GM and Paulo Coelho). Worked for me, not caring about stats!

5. How do you find the blogs to comment?

I look around on Facebook, Google Plus and Triberr for blogs relevant to my digital nomad niche. Then I check to see if the blog has a vibrant community of commenters. I also assess the quality of the blog itself: How is the content? How is the presentation? If a pro runs the blog, I'll comment there because I want to connect with the blogging big dogs.

6. Do you have a list of blogs that you frequently visit to post a comment on any new article? How big is your list?

I've bookmarked over 50 blogs, but some I may only visit once every 2 weeks. Others I may visit twice a week. It depends on both the frequency of posting and who I feel like networking with on any given day.

7. If a new author wants to start

promoting his/her book via blog commenting, where should he/she start? What should be the first step?

Post a comment on *this* blog. Seriously Harsh, you're a wonderfully successful author, and you have such a vibrant, prospering network of blogger/authors around you, that posting a three to four paragraph comment on this post will multiply opportunities for you. My readers will find you, newbie author, and they will help you. So will Harsh's readers. Start with commenting here, and make the comment a whopper, and you'll slowly pop up on reader's radars, and your presence will expand.

8. What are the things one needs to avoid while blog commenting?

Don't do a comment "drive-by." By that, I mean a one sentence comment that was written just to get a backlink or traffic. No good, you lose your reputation as an author or blogger by being this selfish. Use first names, always! Don't comment unless you are willing to personalize things, because using names endears you to your fellow bloggers. My first name is the best sounding word in my native tongue, and most bloggers feel this way.

9. You have been featured on many blogs within a very short amount of time.

What's your secret to getting more interviews? Should an author start with commenting on blogs that accepts interviews from authors?

I gobble up interview requests, completing them quickly, and I post in-depth comments only on authority blogs. I also find, as Lao Tzu's saying goes, "when you seize opportunities, they multiply." I would comment on blogs where you would receive the high level of visibility, whether they are author interview blogs or simply blogs relevant to your niche.

10. What other social networks do you use on a regular basis?

Twitter is number one for me, and I am warming up to Pinterest a lot these days, because the site works so well with my travel images. I also use Facebook and Google Plus regularly.

11. Do you have any tips to promote books via Twitter or Facebook? How can one reach a larger audience?

Promote other authors and bloggers from your niche on Twitter and Facebook and engage with them. Express interest in others, and they'll express interest in you. Notice others and they'll notice you. RT folks from your niche, Facebook Share folks from your niche, and you'll find other authors and bloggers who will do the same for you.

12. Do you use YouTube or Slideshare to promote your work? If yes, which one works better?

I use YouTube, but I'm not as active on that network - trying to find the 25th hour ☺

13. If a reader has any queries, how can he/she reach you?

Any readers can reach me through my blog at Blogging from Paradise, and can also send me an email: rbbidd@gmail.com
Thanks for sharing this opportunity with me, Harsh!

Chapter 5

Embrace Opportunities

You can't imagine how many people let opportunities slip away. If you ask me for a number, it will be above 99%.

What are opportunities?

Opportunities are new doors and windows in our life that open in front of us every day.

It can be as small as an email or as big as talking to 1000 people in a conference. To give you an idea of how opportunities work, let me give you a few examples.

- Thousands of people have surfed through this book on Amazon, but only a handful will buy the book.
- I ran ads before launching this book. I was giving it away for free to all my beta readers. Guess the conversion rate? It was less than 5%. It means 95% of the authors chose not to get this book even for free.
- I invited a lot of authors to do an

interview on FireYourMentor.com. Less than 1% of authors responded. Most of them told me that they had no time. When I checked with the people who agreed to do an interview, all of them were highly successful in life, the reason being that they embraced every opportunity that knocked on their doors.
- I invited Steve Scott to do an interview for this book. He earns $60.000 from his books. He agreed the moment I sent him a PM on Facebook. Are you busier than he is?
- Once a buddy of mine recommended a book called "Millionaire Fastlane." Most people will ignore it as just another book. I took special interest and did my own due research and finally bought it. This book literally changed my life.
- I saw that most books in the niche of "Book Marketing" were focused towards offline marketing, getting on radio, getting in the newspaper, selling more physical copies, etc. I saw an opportunity to write a book that focused on selling more Kindle books via online marketing.
- A couple of months back, I saw a guy offering a book marketing gig. He

promoted third party books to his audience via contests. Most people ignored him because his gig was costly. Moreover it was "too good to be true." I not only tried his service, but also teamed up with him to resell his service by combining it with my audience. A single opportunity helped me make thousands of dollars with absolutely no work.

- I always ask my readers to connect with me directly via email. For every 100 books sold, I get one email, but 99% ignores the opportunity to build a new relationship. If you know me, I am someone who takes a genuine interest in helping people.

I do agree that I am someone who is blind to most opportunities in life, but aren't we all are? Still, if we can grab at least one new opportunity every day, it can change our life forever.

Opportunities wait for none

You should be the first one to grab an opportunity. There are many takers. You need to act fast and act now.

Let me give you a simple example from an instance that happened today in my life. A few weeks back, I brought a Bing ads coupon, but totally forgot to use it. I kept procrastinating that one day I would create a campaign on Bing. Today, I received an email that the coupon expired. BAM! I lost $125 and maybe even a lot more than that in sales and potential leads.

While I was reading a book today, I came up with a new business idea. Either I can procrastinate about it or start taking action right from this very moment. After my previous experience, I think I will set aside two hours each night to work on that new idea. I have learned my lesson already.

Time and tide waits for none. Opportunities are very much time specific. If we can't grab them while they are available, it's going to be too late.

In a broader picture, I am in my mid-20s. If I don't take the opportunity to build and sell a sustainable business right now, I won't have the stream of passive income in my 30s. Similarly, if I don't produce enough books right now, I won't generate enough book royalties in my 30s. The time is now and we should act on it.

Just yesterday, I received an email from a friend who invited me to join a mastermind group. I procrastinated in the beginning, but somewhere along the line I knew that I had nothing to lose if I just gave it a try. I quickly joined soon after that. I was surprised to find similar names of people who were already earning six figures. If I would have let go of this opportunity, I would have lost a golden chance to meet these people and interact directly with them.

Here's my question to you. How many times do you ignore replying to a comment on your blog or ignore an email requesting you to do an interview? When you see a niche website similar to your book, do you try to build a relationship with the blog owner? It takes effort to see results. There's no secret formula. The only secret formula I am aware of is to "TAKE ACTION."

So, if you ask me: "Harsh, is there an opportunity while I am reading this book? If the answer is 'yes,' then why don't I see it?"

Here's my answer: TAKE ACTION.

Leave a review for this book. Connect with me on Twitter and Facebook. Let's build a personal connection. Whenever I send you an email, open it and reply. Come and join my self-publishing forum on http://fireyourmentor.com/forums/. If I have a book marketing service to sell, instead of ignoring it, try to see the value behind it.

There's an opportunity every step of the way. We miss them because we choose to ignore them consciously.

There's no magic audience. Anybody who is a human being might read your book.

I approach a lot of authors to interview for FireYourMentor.com. The most common explanation for rejection is, "I don't think your audience will read my book." Seriously?

How can one possibly think that a person who reads self-help books won't read science fiction? A reader is a reader. Of course there are some people who will only read a particular genre, but the majority of them will read books on almost any genre/niche.

I read business books, motivational books, philosophy, psychology, recipes, diet, fitness, science fiction and a lot more. Just because I mostly read business books doesn't mean I do not read any other books. It's like assuming that people who watch action movies do not watch drama.

For any author, there's no magic audience. Exploit any opportunity you get to get the word about your book out there. Do not ignore an opportunity only because you think people won't find your book suitable.

Let's say you are an author who has written a book on "Developing good habits." If you get a chance to interview on a site about football, would you ignore it?

Even though it's not your niche, you should understand that some football players might want to develop some good habits. In fact, serious sportspersons are extremely disciplined. They might in fact be your ideal audience.

Unless you are a celebrity author, read this paragraph twice.

I can name hundreds of authors who ignored opportunities to do a radio interview or a blog interview, to participate in a mastermind group, to guest post or speak to an audience (both online and offline).

Yeah, I know there are authors who will say that they never received such an opportunity. WAKE UP!

What if you weren't invited to be on the radio? Go to Fiverr and you will find over 50 people selling radio advertisements for $5.00.

You might not have been invited to do a written interview on a blog, but have you ever contacted any blogger yourself? **You cannot expect people to find you if you don't show up.**

What if you weren't invited to be a part of a

mastermind group? PM a few Facebook friends and create a mastermind group right now.

Maybe no one ever invited you to write a guest post, but why don't you contact them first? **Google:** "Write for us" and you will see all of the opportunities lying in front of you. You can also contact two or three of your closest friends who maintain a blog and show your interest in writing a guest article. You have to start somewhere.

You might not be famous enough yet to receive an invitation for a speaking engagement, but why don't you exploit YouTube which is absolutely FREE? Why don't you have a channel yet?

There are numerous opportunities in front of us; yet we think that we are the unfortunate souls who are not as lucky as the celebrity authors.

I don't know about anybody else, so I will talk about myself. Whenever I feel that the world hasn't rewarded me with opportunities for quite some time now, I tell myself that I am the one who hasn't exploited all the options available in front of me. Maybe I was too afraid to take an unknown step. It was my lack of commitment and dedication. I can't blame the world for it. It's such an amazing approach. Once I realize that I was the one who hadn't explored, opportunities started appearing magically. Try it.

Chapter 6

Go Direct

Oh no, not another chapter on "Capturing email addresses." I know, I know. By now you already know the value of capturing email addresses. I am not going to tell you why you should capture email addresses. This chapter is dedicated toward what happens next, after you have captured email addresses. This is where the real marketing begins.

Create a supporting product

Ask any clever book marketer and they will show you their supporting product. A supporting product is a bonus that you can give away along with your book.

The supporting product should have some value. If it's valueless, nobody will give a damn about it. Exceed expectations and you will be able to win your readers.

Steve Scott is a well-known writer among indie authors. So, let me give you his example. If you check out his "habit" books under "S J Scott," you will see that with each and every book, there is a free gift. The free gift is actually an Ebook in PDF format. It's not a 200 page booklet. He offers value even with his supporting products. It's a 12,000 page Ebook, which is almost equivalent to the length of his paid books.

I try to follow a very simple technique. I give away the audiobook for free. I know I could have earned a few dollars if I sell the audiobook, but when I give it away for free, I am giving away immense value along with the digital/paperback version. It's easy to grab the email addresses of your readers that way.

If you are a non-native speaker, hire a voiceover artist. It might be costly, but if you have the budget, go ahead with the plan. For people with a limited budget, invest in a good voiceover software. You can buy software from www.ivona.com, which is also an Amazon-owned company. It can also get the job done.

So, what other supporting products can you offer along with your book?

You can offer another book in PDF format as a free gift. You can provide the audiobook, a free Amazon gift card, a mega discount on your other books, a free consultation, a free webinar, a free course or a lucky draw. Anything that's free will attract attention.

I have tried giving away a lot of things, but the things that have worked best for me are free Ebooks, courses, gift cards and audiobooks.

It also depends on the niche you are working on. If you are a children's book author, you can giveaway some free games, puzzles or an app. If you are a business author, you can provide a free workbook or a productivity app along with your book. Think hard and you will come up with something. Yeah, think right now. Take a five minute break. Grab a pen and a piece of paper. Write down ten items you can give away for free along with your book. Once you have written them down, you can get back to reading your book.

Reaching an audience directly

Amazon is the world's largest bookstore and you do enjoy a lot of benefits if you are loyal to Amazon. But if you are not enrolled under KDP Select, then you can promote your digital version elsewhere as well.

https://gumroad.com and https://selz.com are two websites that you can use if you want to go direct. You can list your Ebooks on these sites and drive traffic using advertising or blogging. You get to keep 100% of your royalties, unlike on Amazon.

The best part is not the extra profit on royalty, but the ability to capture your buyers' contact info. Amazon doesn't show your reader's contact info and thus you cannot re-target your old readers. But when you go direct, you have the ability to re-target your old readers again and again.

There's a negative side to going direct. You will have to do all the selling. You are solely responsible for driving traffic to your product page. If you have a blog, a YouTube channel, a podcast or an already established audience, going direct is the most preferable route.

Creating a sales funnel is important

Try creating Facebook ads to sell your digital books, and look at the ROI. It will most probably be negative, the reason being that you haven't created a sales funnel yet.

Think about it for a second.

When you run a Facebook ad to a U.S.A. audience, it will cost you approximately $0.5 to $1.00 per click. If you are selling your Ebook for $10.00, then you must get at least one sale for every ten to 20 clicks. This is a very high expectation to begin with. Most people on Facebook are in the surfing mode and not in the buying mode. Do you think they will hold a credit card while on Facebook? They are probably taking a loo while surfing through Facebook on their mobile.

A reasonable conversion rate will be anywhere between 0.5% to 3%. Let's assume you spend $0.5 per click. This means that for every $50.00 you spend on Facebook, you will make three sales for a profit of $30.00 (if you sell each Ebook for $10). It's a negative $20.00 in ROI.

However, what if you give away freebies instead of trying to sell them on your first interaction? The conversion rate can go as high as 15% to 20% if you are giving away a freebie. So, for every $50.00 spent, you can capture 15 to 20 email addresses. If you can get three people to buy your book, you will earn $30.00. You can retarget these three people again and ask them to buy your second book. You will earn another $30.00. You have already made a positive ROI of $10.00. This is called a sales funnel.

You can send them an email and ask them to buy your book. A few days later, you can ask them to buy another book. You can sell them one product after another. A reader who has read your first book is more likely to buy your second book.

Of course, don't forget that you will have to first build a relationship with your email subscribers before selling them anything.

Alright, I talked about paid advertising to reach an audience, but there are a lot of free ways to do it as well.

Let me tell you a story.

Long ago, there was a king called Kenneth in 15th Century Scotland. His kingdom was small, but prosperous. He had skilled laborers, good rainfall and harvested massive agricultural output. His kingdom was also rich in natural resources, including precious minerals like gold and silver. One day, a king from a neighboring kingdom pronounced war against his kingdom. With a small army, it was almost certain that he would lose this war.

King Kenneth went out looking for allies. Ultimately, he found three kings with a huge army to help him in this war, but he was asked to sign a treaty. The treaty stated that King Kenneth would have to pay them 50% revenue from the overall tax income for one whole year. He agreed and formed a pact. Ultimately he won the war with the help of his allies.

Smart marketers are using the same technique from this very early time to promote their products. You form allies with people with a big audience.

If you don't have a big audience, it's alright. Go out looking for people who already have a big audience. If money is not an issue for you, then where's the first place you would go out looking for an audience? Google and Facebook, right?

Similarly, there are other website owners who have a large audience. Think about all the forums in your niche. Each forum has thousands of members.

I moderated two webmaster forums back in 2007. I know a little inside story. Most forums do not make any money. They do monetize via Adsense and other sponsors, but most of the time it's not even enough to support their hosting fees.

No doubt, some forums are immensely successful, but most forums aren't. They have a huge unused asset (their audience). If you show them that you can help them earn revenue from their existing audience, they will be more than happy to accept your offer.

Again, it's obvious that you will have to face more than a 90% rejection, but that's alright. It's not that you didn't pitch them well or something's wrong with your book. It's not your fault at all. They will ignore or reject your proposal because 90% of the people are blind when an opportunity knocks on their door.

Similarly, you can also contact blog owners. It's a little difficult to get your proposal accepted by a blog owner because a blogger with a good audience already makes a lot of money. Moreover, they find a lot of sponsors who pay them hundreds of dollars to place a banner on their site.

You will need a different approach with bloggers - a simple email stating, "Hey I want you to promote my book with your audience and we will share 50% revenue" won't do the job. These bloggers probably get hundreds of such emails every month. The big question is how do you stand out? Do you remember the power of "blog commenting" that I talked about in my previous chapters? Use your secret weapon to stand out of the crowd. If a blogger see you commenting on each and every article he/she has written for one whole month, there's a very good chance that they might accept your proposal. The psychology of reciprocity will automatically play its magic.

Revenue Share or Giveaway?

Most blog owners are reluctant to promote a third party product to their loyal fans. You might want to pitch them differently, rather than asking them to spam their audience with an offer.

In such cases, you can approach them to host a giveaway to their audience. There's a lot of competition even with giveaways. I know a couple of bloggers who have told me that they get four to five emails every week from authors who request them to host a giveaway on their blog.

It's up to you and your intelligence to stand out from the crowd. I recommend using blog commenting to build a relationship with the blog owner first. You can also start tweeting and liking every article posted by that owner to build a relationship. If you can come up with any new and unique idea, use it. You know how you can promote your book, but to get there you need to do the hard work.

Giveaways can go viral if done correctly. You can also capture email addresses using giveaways. There's no direct correlation with sales from a giveaway, but just think about it for a second. When a participant comes across your giveaway, he/she will share it on social media. Thus, it will reach a wider audience. Think of giveaways as a way to brand yourself.

They might not buy your book while they wait for the giveaway results, but when they visit your product page, Amazon will store cookies on their computers. Amazon does a great job of promoting books to its visitors. They send email reminders and also display books in multiple categories inside Amazon. These visitors will easily recognize your book the next time they surf through Amazon. This is just another example of how to create a sales funnel inside Amazon. You might not get a customer on the first day, but eventually you will sell more books.

Quick lesson to go direct via Twitter, Facebook, and Pinterest

There are enough books on social media marketing. I am not going to get into details. I will assume that you are already aware of these three popular social media networks. I would recommend you read my book, *Engagement Interaction Conversion,* if you want to see more of the details on this.

I won't talk about the traditional tips and techniques people use with social media. I will only tell you what has worked for me. I am a man of automation, so most of my techniques will involve software. If you want to do it manually instead, that's up to you. Alright, let's get started.

Twitter:

The idea behind Twitter is simple. If you follow someone on Twitter, they follow you back. Now, we will use this concept to gain a laser-targeted follower base. I use a software called "Tweet Adder." Download my PDF guide (http://getaccess.me/tweet-adder-abm) to learn how to use it.

I will track down authors who write books in my niche/genre. I will sort his followers based on activity and engagement. Then, I will start following his followers one after the other. I keep it limited to 100 followers every day. A percentage of these followers will follow you back. The software "Tweet Adder" has a facility where you can check for people who are not following you back. I give them four to five days and after that, I unfollow everyone who didn't follow me back.

After a few months you should have a base of highly targeted followers who were are following other famous authors in your niche. It's a nice way of building your fan base from zero.

One you are done collecting Twitter followers, it's now your job to engage with them. Tweet and reply to tweets that you like. As you start a conversation, they will come to know more about you. The rule of reciprocity will start playing its role now (wow, this rule again!). As you retweet their tweets, they will start retweeting yours. It will expose you to their followers and you will slowly start gaining more and more followers.

Here's what I recommend:

Have a pinned tweet that links to your book. Check out mine:

Anybody who visits your Twitter profile will see this pinned tweet. This will give even more exposure to your books.

There's a place to post your website on Twitter. My recommendation is to link it to your author page. That way, people who visit your Twitter profile can read your bio. It also opens you up to more interview and guest blogging opportunities in the future.

Harshajyoti Das
@jr_sci

Bestselling Author of 3 books.
Entrepreneur. CEO. Traveler and a
Business Coach.

○ India
⌘ Harsh.im
⊙ Joined May 2009

Pinterest:

Pinterest is so viral that you will receive traffic from a pin that you have made months back. Don't believe me? Let me show you an example. Here's a screenshot of my traffic stats from Pinterest to my book, *No SEO Forever*. I stopped pinning about two months back, but I still receive 20 to 50 visitors daily from Pinterest.

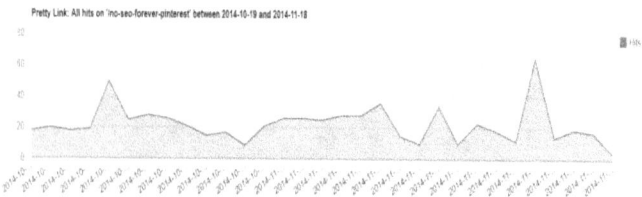

Once, I received 1000 visitors within 24 hours. Here's the screenshot.

Tracking ID	Clicks	Items Ordered	Items Shipped	Shipped Items Revenue	Advertising Fees
penigmabookstore-20	4	0	0	$0.00	$0.00
pinterest0a6d-20	948	0	0	$0.00	$0.00
TOTALS	952	0	0	$0.00	$0.00

Pinterest can be more powerful than Facebook or Twitter because it's filled with pictures, but not text. The likelihood of an image going viral is a thousand times more than a text message. That makes Pinterest our most preferred candidate for direct traffic.

How do I earn traffic from Pinterest? How long does it take?

For me, it takes less than five minutes to set up my Pinterest software. The software does its job while I am sleeping.

If you want to do it manually, it's up to you. Or, you can hire a VA to do it for you. The bottom line is, don't let this opportunity slip away. Who knows how long Pinterest will be around?

I have interviewed Matt Stone, an author, a publisher and a brilliant marketers. Let's hear it from him.

1. **Matt, according to you what is the single most essential component or strategy for authors when it comes to marketing?**

The most important thing is building a list of highly-engaged email subscribers, but I honestly am just as turned off by the word "marketing" as most authors are. To me, marketing means advertising means commercials mean blah. As authors, we should hold ourselves to a higher standard than your typical spammer and internet huckster. I can't say enough about the importance of building a subscriber list, treating them like your best friends, and using that list to help your books launch harder and perform better. Aside from that, very little "marketing" should be done. Start writing that next book.

2. **Most authors do not maintain an email list. What do you want to say to them?**

It's really important to be able to communicate intimately with your fans on demand. Not only is it a great way for them to get to know you more personally and build a stronger bond with your work, but those initial downloads and reviews (your best fans will always give you better reviews than the general public) in the first few days are the most important thing for having a successful run with an eBook—at least with the way Amazon currently works. There are dozens of other advantages, such as getting affiliate commission when you promote your book to email subscribers, getting more $50 bounties from Audible, giving away review copies, doing market research, and the "list" goes on.

3. How can an author collect emails? What are some of the best strategies?

The most important thing is to create one or several "lead pages." Lead pages only give visitors two options—to subscribe or leave. With this setup, usually 5-50% of the visitors that arrive on your site will subscribe depending on where they came from and how well your lead page performs in general. A simple one-page website with three sentences placed over a stock image can perform phenomenally well. No need to blog your fingers to the bone or have a complicated, expensive site. I've helped create several author sites that convert just fine and took just 1-2 hours to create. Something like this is all you need to start building a list: http://mattstonebooks.com

4. **How important is a book launch? What are the steps or pre-requisites one needs to follow to have a successful launch?**

I'd say the launch is at least 80% of a book's success. Nothing matters more. If you have an email list built, then you don't have to do much to have a successful launch—just release it at 99 cents to your loyal followers and try to get as many downloads as possible at launch. If you don't have a list, you're going to have to network with others in your niche/genre that have a list built up and form some kind of mutually-beneficial alliance. You may have to send out lots of copies to bloggers and reviewers. You may have to pay these people to promote your book. You may have to drop money on advertising of some kind. Whatever you do, make sure you get at least 100 downloads in the first 48 hours if you want your book to be successful. That isn't a guarantee that your book will be a hit, but if you don't get those initial 100 downloads, that's a guarantee that your book won't ever get off the ground. And 100 is the minimum. Serious authors should really be shooting for at least 1,000.

5. **Let's assume that an author has published his book in 2011. Now, what can he do to re-launch or bring back some buzz around his book?**

Flash sales and book promotions are the most likely to bring it back to life, but the effects probably won't last that long. Another effective strategy is to write a new book, give it a big launch, and have it topping charts. That will breathe some life back into it as well. If the book has never sold that well, you're better off unpublishing it, making some changes to the cover, title, book description, and content, and trying again—this time with the proper amount of launch pressure built up.

6. Do you suggest that an author should maintain his blog? For a fiction writer it becomes more difficult to write blog posts.

If your only goal is to be a successful author, you shouldn't waste time blogging. If you do write blog posts and articles, they should be posted on someone else's site—putting your work in front of new eyes—and driving leads back to a high-performing lead page on your site. I'm so adamant about this I write under the pen name "Buck Flogging" and have written a book about this called *Kill Your Blog*, haha.

7. I know you have had some experience with traditional publishers as well. Why do you support self-publishing? Would love to get some comparative statistics if any.

Traditional publishing is just unnecessary. In the modern world, traditional publishers can't do that much to sell your book. What works well in digital publishing typically isn't performed by traditional publishers, who will catabolize eBook sales in favor of selling hardcopies. They still sell physical copies quite well, but the big money is shifting to successful eBook sellers, and that trend isn't going to change. I just got my first check for six months of sales on a traditionally-published book. It totalled $3,500, which is below average for the first six months on books that I've released to my current fanbase. The difference is that a monumental amount of effort and expenditure went into the production and release of the traditionally-published book, and it took six months to get published from the day I sent in the manuscript vs. a few weeks with a self-published title.

8. Could you shed some light on foreign language translations? How profitable are they? Are they as big as the US and UK markets? Would love some statistics if you are comfortable.

I got lucky with my first translated book. It was a French translation of my bestselling book, and it brought in around $1,100 in its first quarter. Sales have since sloughed off to around $150 per month. I've also published a book in Spanish, and that was a total flop—totalling only $20-30 in its first two months. There is great promise here, but my exploration into it is very preliminary right now. I'd love to put a team together to focus just on foreign book sales—figuring out a way to crack the code and make foreign translation worth the time and money spent to make it happen.

9. Last but not the least, how can your publishing company, Archangel Ink, help authors to sell more books?

The company technically belongs to my partner Rob Archangel, (Yes, that's really his name!) although I was the leader in developing it and still play a large role in its evolution as a company. The primary function of Archangel Ink is to allow authors to focus more on the writing and less on the editing, formatting, proofreading, cover creation, book description, marketing, audiobook narration, etc. We do all that for the authors. As an author myself, it's quite a luxury, and one that frees up a lot of time to write books or pursue other ventures. However, we also promote our in-house published titles repeatedly through Buck Books (my company, www.buckbooks.net), which we expect to become the most powerful book promotion platform in the world in the next couple of years. After five months, it's arguably the world's 2nd most powerful book promotion entity, especially for nonfiction. So it's looking like we'll be able to not only provide this great service but sell the pants off of just about any book in the not-too-distant future.

10. Any last piece of advice for authors or anything I might have missed?

Focus on growth and not raw numbers. When I started pursuing writing as a full-time career, my numbers were initially quite small. Just $400 per month my first year of selling books. The next year I made close to $2,000 per month. Almost 500% growth. My girlfriend at the time said to me, "Clearly what you're doing isn't working. You need to do something else." But I wasn't deterred at all. My thought process was simply that my business had grown by 500% in a year, that it was working great, and that I should change nothing. I kept at it, and it kept growing steadily, doubling for the next three years, at which point I took time off from writing to focus on publishing, book promotion, and other online endeavors.

Sell that first book and make that first dollar. Then work on achieving slow and steady growth. Most importantly, keep it fun. To really last long enough to make it to the point of having real success with anything you do, you have to love doing it.

Chapter 7

Pre-Launch Marketing

What will happen if the army goes to a war with absolutely no training and preparation? You need all the training before going to war. You need to equip yourself with armor, bullet-proof vests and other gear.

Preparing a launch is somewhat similar. You cannot launch your book without preparation. You need a full pre-launch marketing strategy before a book launch.

When I say strategy, there can be "n" numbers of strategies. If you have a big budget, you can call a celebrity to inaugurate your book. You will get big media attention. However, we are talking about online marketing here, especially for Indie authors who work on a very limited budget.

Before I go any further, I know you must be wondering if I have done any massive book launches for my own books. **There are many people who would tell you "Do as I say." But, I prefer to say, "Do as I have done."**

Here are a few screenshots of my book launches:

Product Details

File Size: 1665 KB

Print Length: 216 pages

Sold by: Amazon Digital Services, Inc.

Language: English

ASIN: B00J4TR7W2

Text-to-Speech: Enabled

X-Ray: Not Enabled

Word Wise: Not Enabled

Lending: Enabled

Amazon Best Sellers Rank: #642 Paid in Kindle Store (See Top 100 Paid in Kindle Store)
  #1 in Kindle Store > Kindle eBooks > **Computers & Technology**
  #1 in Books > Business & Money > Marketing & Sales > Marketing > **Web Marketing**
  #1 in Kindle Store > Kindle eBooks > Business & Money > Marketing & Sales > Marketing > **Web Marketing**

Product Details

File Size: 1314 KB

Print Length: 109 pages

Simultaneous Device Usage: Unlimited

Publisher: Anuj Publishing; 1st edition (September 22, 2014)

Sold by: Amazon Digital Services, Inc.

Language: English

ASIN: B00NTQ7ON2

Text-to-Speech: Enabled

X-Ray: Not Enabled

Lending: Enabled

Amazon Best Sellers Rank: #1,593 Paid in Kindle Store (See Top 100 Paid in Kindle Store)
  #2 in Kindle Store > Kindle eBooks > Business & Money > Marketing & Sales > **Sales & Selling**
  #3 in Kindle Store > Kindle eBooks > Business & Money > Industries > **E-commerce**
  #3 in Kindle Store > Kindle eBooks > Business & Money > Marketing & Sales > Marketing > **Web Marketing**

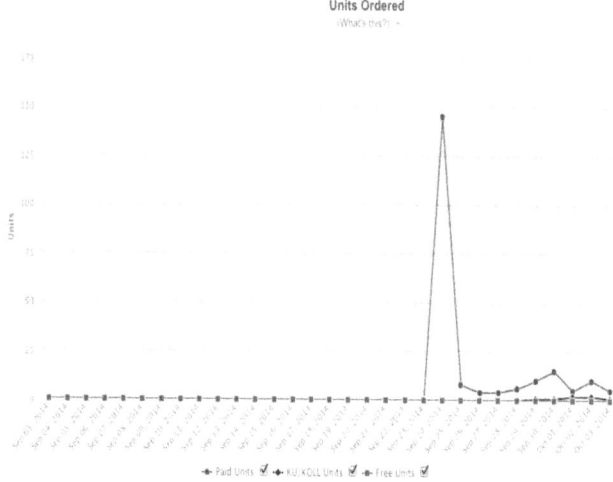

Do you know what my number one weapon was for these massive launches? The answer is "EMAIL MARKETING." You have read about it everywhere. Many people have already told you about it. Still, there are plenty of authors who haven't harnessed the power of email marketing.

A weapon without a detonator is just a toy. Having a weapon doesn't help. You need to know how to use it.

There's Facebook and there's Twitter, but nothing works like email marketing. If you haven't built an email list yet, start doing it now. Don't wait. Take a break from this book and open an account with Aweber. For every minute you procrastinate, you are losing an opportunity.

How many email subscribers do I need?

There is no definite answer to this. If you have 10,000 email subscribers and none of them are your "true fans." it's a useless list. You need "true fans" that will go out of their way to help you.

Even if you have 100 people on your email list who are dedicated, whom you have personally connected with, who are not just email subscribers but your friends, I think that is enough for a good launch.

When it comes to an email list, it's not the quantity that matters, it's the quality.

Look for interview opportunities on various blogs:

Just one or two months before the launch, try to find interview opportunities in some popular blogs in your niche.

Getting interviewed is not enough. It's just like "raw materials" for building a house. You need to know how to use these "raw materials" so that you can build your house. Let me walk you through the "process" or "sales funnel" behind getting interviewed.

The main goal in getting interviewed is not to build your authority, but to reach an audience.

You will be exposed to an audience and now it's your duty to invite each and every one of them to become your audience.

Getting interviewed is not the end but the beginning.

How do you invite them to become your audience?

The interview will do half of your job. They will know you from your interview. I will say this again - do not try to sell anything in an interview. It's not worth it. When you are being interviewed, reveal yourself to an unknown audience so that they are able to know you. Reveal how you think and function. They need to know you before they can trust you.

Once they know you, invite them to join your tribe (or your audience). Ask them for their email ID in exchange for a few free chapters. Yes, again it comes to "grabbing their emails." That's how you stay in touch with the online world, right?

There's no point in asking them to like your page or asking them to follow you on Twitter. You can do that later via email.

I recommend giving away 25 to 30 copies of your

digital copy for free to an unknown audience whenever you get interviewed. Just ask them to fill out a form and you will choose them on a first-come, first-serve basis. It will literally cost you nothing for this promotion, but the upside is huge.

Your email should be short and precise. Nobody has the time to go through a long email. Bloggers and editors are immensely busy. They will hardly spend three seconds per email. You have just three seconds to grab their attention. If you send a long email, it's most likely going to be ignored.

I send an email from my email ID: press@harsh.im. It looks professional when you use a dedicated private email address for press inquiries.

Here's a sample interview request that I usually send to newspapers/magazines/blogs:

Sub: Looking for an interview opportunity

To,

The Editor,
XYZ Newspaper

Hello,

I am an Indie author. I publish my books with Amazon. So far, I have published eight bestselling books. I would love to appear for an interview on your esteemed journal. I can talk about the evolving self-publishing industry, the rise of digital books and book marketing.

You can send me your questions via email and I will reply within a day or two.

For more information, visit: http://Harsh.Im

Thank You!

Regards,
Harshajyoti Das

In my second chapter I talked about setting up an author's website. This is where it comes into play. You needn't send them a bunch of links to your Twitter profile, Facebook page, Amazon author page, previous interviews, etc. A link to your author website is enough. It's short, clean and shows that you are a brand.

Alright, it's time for a coffee break (both for you and me). Get yourself a cup of coffee. Find ten newspapers or magazines in your city and send them this very email. Personalize it as per your requirements. Reading this book without taking actions will do you no good. **TAKE ACTION**. I am here to show you how I market my books, but I need your commitment to take action at the same time.

Please, take a 15 minute break. Grab a cup of coffee and send ten cold emails.

Please be assured that sometimes the rejection rate will be 99%. So, unless and until you have sent 100 emails, don't be disheartened.

Oh, I know your next question. Where do I find these newspapers and magazines? My first answer is to Google them. But if you want me to spoon feed you, here's the link to a website a list of over 12,000 newspapers from across the globe. http://www.thepaperboy.com/. To make it even easier for you, I have compiled a list of 158 email addresses of all the major newspapers in the U.S. You can find that list here:
http://pastebin.com/raw.php?i=mkvvtHQt

A little bit of motivation for you:

What's 1% of 12,000? It's 120. If you contact 12,000 newspapers, you can be almost 100% assured that you will get interviewed in over 100 newspapers. Assuming each local newspaper has at least a minimum audience of 10,000, you will have access to over 100,000 people. If your acceptance rate goes up from 1% to 2% and the rejection rate comes down from 99% to 98%, you will be exposed to an audience of over 200,000. How is that for a little motivation?

Alright now, go and make your first ten cold emails. You can catch me after a 15 minute coffee break. We will break some myths about blog tours when you come back.

Guest post like a rock star

This is somewhat optional since it requires a little bit of time and effort. You don't need to guest post on 50 blogs. Don't listen when someone says that you need to guest post in a number of places. I will tell you why.

First, if you are writing a guest post, you need to write a well-researched article with 2000 to 5000 words. We are talking about a big fat article here. There are numerous 500 words articles and the internet is filled with them. The average lifetime of a blog post is one day. So, we need to make an impact with our article, an article which will be shared and liked by many, extending its lifetime.

Secondly, many blogs do not have much traffic. People talk about going to do blog tours, but I have seen marketers misleading authors to blog tour on a couple of blogspot blogs with no real traffic. Marketers do it for the money and innocent authors fall prey to their cheap promotional offers. Many marketers will often ask authors to submit the same interview to a number of other blogspot blogs. They call it "Blog Tour." I call it "Bullshit."

How can you even expect a blog to be termed a "quality blog" if they accept duplicate content? I know there are a lot of syndicated news sites, but they are already huge. They have an Alexa rank of less than 1000, whereas these Blogspot/Wordpress blogs are hosted on free platforms. The owner doesn't even have the money to invest in a domain name or a logo. How can you even think that it's going to help you promote your books? (Alexa.com is an analytical platform that determines the popularity of any website in terms of traffic).

For authors who aren't aware, Google penalizes for duplicate content. Any blog that accepts duplicate interviews, book descriptions are not loved by Google. Now, it may be true that they get traffic from sources other than Google, but I highly doubt it. If they do not have the money to invest in a .com domain name, do you think they will invest in Facebook ads?

You should look out for big blogs with an Alexa rank of 50,000 or less. If by any chance you get the opportunity to post on a blog with a huge amount of traffic (think Alexa top 2000 site), you don't need to waste your time looking for more blogs. Just make an impact on this one blog. Devote all your energy into writing one of the best articles ever published on their site.

The signature or the author bio is really important. Any blog will allow authors to post a short bio about themselves below their article. Here's what a good and a bad author bio looks like:

Bad author bio:

John Doe is the author of Magical Island, a fantasy novel. He is a bestselling author of four novels. He graduated from UCLA and is a state-level chess champion. You can get in touch with him at https://twitter.com/johndoe

Here's what a good author bio looks like:

John Doe is the author of Magical Island, a fantasy novel. He is a bestselling author of four novels. Grab the first six chapters of his upcoming novel here: www.magicalisland.com/private-content .

I will tell you what makes a bad and a good author bio. Cut your bio short and remove anything that doesn't talk about your book. How is being a state-level chess champion related to you getting more email subscribers? Your author bio should have a clear CTA (call to action). You want their email address and in return you are giving them something for free. It's as simple as that.

Brand yourself. Get a .com domain name for your book. Use psychological hooks to make them even more interested. See how we have used "private-content" instead of "free-chapters."

Don't ask them to follow you on Twitter at first. You can do that even a week later by sending them an email. Prioritize your actions every step of the way.

Get some editorial reviews by sending a .pdf copy

We have already talked about making friends with influencers with the help of blog commenting. You can leverage your connection to get some editorial reviews.

Just before the launch date, email a couple of influencers in your niche with a PDF copy. Thank them for motivating you with their articles. I do not recommend asking for a review directly. Instead, tell them that they can have the digital copy for free. Reviews are not mandatory, but if they want to review it, it's highly appreciated.

When you give them the freedom to choose whether to review or not, they usually respond positively.

Contact Newspapers and Magazines for an editorial review:

This is usually tougher than contacting bloggers, especially for an Indie author, but here's a small trick. Almost all the magazines and newspapers are in digital format. Most of them also have an option to leave a blog comment. Follow the steps to build a connection with an editor or a journalist.

1. Google the term: *Review of bestselling book*
2. Visit the website of a magazine/newspaper you want to appear on
3. Start blog commenting two months before the launch date

We will again use the "powerful magical weapon" of blog commenting to build new connections. If an editor/journalist/moderator sees your name repeatedly for two months, they will become familiar with your name. When you send them a PDF copy for a book review, chances are they will immediately recognize you. Your odds of getting rejected come down from

99% to below 50%.

Start your blog commenting spree

Pre-launch period is the best period to start your blog commenting spree. You will have enough time to filter out the sites you want to hang around.

I have already talked about blog commenting before. I won't talk about it again. Let's move on to the next strategy.

Q&A Session on Twitter/Facebook groups, along with an influencer

There are numerous opportunities on Twitter and Facebook, apart from just connecting with your friends and followers. One of them is to host a Q&A session. If you have an audience, you can host a Q&A session yourself.

However, if you do not have a massive audience then you can team up with an influencer and co-host a Q&A session. An example of such a Q&A session is #indiechat. It's hosted by bibliocrunch.com. They host a Q&A session with an author every Tuesday. Similarly, there are others who host Q&A sessions regularly.

Google Hangouts can also prove to be useful. There are many authors who will host weekly hangouts on a certain topic.

The idea behind these Q&A sessions is to throw yourself out there. Get a little uncomfortable and break your invisible fences. When people see you everywhere, they will recognize your book. But apart from visibility, there's something more important.

You are providing content and value to somebody. In a way, you are helping a fellow influencer by creating a product out of thin air. Think about it this way - when you appear for a Q&A chat on Twitter, you are promoting his brand. When someone sits with you to create a video interview with you, they are creating a product. They earn revenues from sponsors, advertisements and leads. If they post that interview on YouTube, it will again drive traffic to their website. Ultimately, you are helping them create a product out of thin air.

When you help someone in their business, you build a relationship with them. You build allies who will also help you when the time comes. Remember the story of King Kenneth? In order to save his kingdom, he had to form allies. It's actually easier to succeed when you have many helping hands instead of just two.

Dominate a #Hashtag on Twitter

Find out the popular #hashtags in your niche/genre. Let's say for me it's #bookmarketing. There are other hashtags, such as #amwriting. I'll tell you what, let me give you a complete list of all the hashtags. I did my research and found about 100 hashtags that an author can use.

List of hashtags to connect with other authors:

- #WriteChat
- #AmRevising
- #RomanceWriter
- #EditGoal
- #WritersBlock
- #WIP
- #1K1H (write one thousand words in one hour)
- #WW
- #WritersLife
- #WriteMotivation
- #WordCount
- #IndieAuthor
- #CopyWriting
- #WriteGoal
- #WroteToday
- #AmEditing
- #ScriptChat

- #WritingBlitz
- #Editing
- #NaNoWriMo (National Novel Writing Month, which is held every November)
- #WriterWednesday
- #MyWANA (writer's community created by Kirsten Lamb)
- #WritingPrompt
- #AmWriting
- #Writing

Popular Hashtags about reading, books, etc:

- #BookWorm
- #MustRead
- #Storytelling
- #IndieThursday
- #WhatToRead
- #GreatReads
- #Books
- #Novel
- #Paperbacks

Hashtags related to the publishing Industry:

- #AskAuthor
- #Publishing

- #IAN1 (Independent Author Network)
- #PromoTip
- #AskAgent
- #SelfPublishing
- #WriteTip
- #AskEditor
- #IndiePub
- #WritingTip
- #BookMarketing
- #BookMarket
- #GetPublished

Genre/niche-specific Hashtags:

- #LitFic
- #Mystery
- #SteamPunk
- #Suspense
- #FaithLitChat
- #UrbanFantasy
- #Erotica
- #YA
- #Poetry
- #Crime
- #Dystopian
- #140Poem
- #YALit
- #KidLitChat

- #WomensFiction
- #TrueStories
- #DarkFantasy
- #HistFic
- #Paranormal
- #Romantic
- #SciFiChat
- #Literature
- #Comedy
- #NonFiction
- #ShortStory
- #Historical
- #MGLit (middle grades literature)
- #MemoirChat
- #RomanticSuspence
- #ScienceFiction
- #PoetryMonth (Each April in the USA)

Promotional hashtags:

- #99c
- #99centsbook
- #AuthorRT
- #BookGiveaway
- #BookMarketing
- #FollowFriday
- #FreebieFriday
- #FreeReads

- #Bookpromotion

- #FreeKindle
- #Freebook
- #Novelines (to quote your own work)

Just pick any random #Hashtag. Copy/paste it on Twitter search and check out the latest tweets. Retweet, reply, favorite and connect with these members. Set aside ten to 15 minutes every day to regularly interact with an audience for a particular hashtag. Rinse and repeat.

Within a couple of weeks, people will start recognizing you for your contributions. You will build new relationships. Some of them will even follow you and retweet your tweets, which will expose you to their audience.

Once you get started, don't stop. If you are too busy to do it yourself, hire a VA to handle your social media marketing. Teach him/her the process and they will do the hard work for you. You can easily hire a VA from Asia for $2.00 per hour.

Join hands with an influencer on YouTube/Google+ for a hangout

When you do not have an audience, you need to form an alliance with other authors. Google+ hangouts are a popular destination for hosting webinars. It's easy to publish them on YouTube, and as you already know, YouTube is the world's second largest search engine after Google. Your videos will receive a lot of views organically, even without any promotions.

You can also find popular YouTube channels and contact the owner. You can pitch to host a webinar or a Q&A session on their YouTube channel. You will invest your time to provide value to their viewers. If you can pitch it to the right person after building a relationship with them, you shouldn't have a problem getting accepted to be featured on their channel. You can use the comment section on YouTube to post your comments to build a connection just like you would have done with blog commenting.

It's easy to find an influencer on YouTube. Just search for the "keyword" and sort out the videos based on popularity/views.

Build fans and followers before publishing your book

It's extremely important that you have an audience before you launch your book. I have already talked about it previously. I will keep this short. At first, build an email list. When I say fans and followers, I do not mean on Facebook and on Twitter. I am talking about building an email list of fans.

I do not discourage building a fan base on Facebook and Twitter, but it should be your second priority. Facebook and Twitter can be a powerful tool to promote your book by word of mouth. Your reach can increase exponentially overnight.

Don't confuse yourself with all these platforms. First, build an email list. Then ask your audience to like you on Facebook and follow you on Twitter. Once they do, interact with them regularly.

With Twitter, I have talked about dominating a #hashtag in my previous strategy. You will receive a lot of profile views when you are seen interacting. Your job is to capture a Twitter view. Your pinned tweet will do the job here. It will have a link to your landing page/opt-in page. When anybody visits your Twitter profile, they will most likely retweet your pinned post and opt in to your email list.

Team up with influencers to promote on their list

Other authors are not competitors but your friends. They can team up to host an event or promote individual books to each other's audiences. If a reader wants to buy a Sci-Fi book, he is most likely to buy more than one book.

When I was doing my research before writing this book, I bought not one but a lot of books on marketing and psychology. Most of the books that I bought were from Amazon from the suggested category, "Customers Who Bought This Item Also Bought."

Readers make many purchasing decisions when a person he/she trusts recommends a particular book. When your book is recommended by an author to their fans, they are most likely to buy it without giving it a second thought. The same is the case when you recommend someone else's book to your fans. They will buy it immediately. It's a win-win scenario for all the authors when they team up.

There are some do's and don'ts associated with this strategy.

If you don't know an author, do not send them a cold email asking to cross promote each other's books. They will freak out and will delete your email without giving it a second thought. At first, build a connection. (Oh no! Don't tell me again about connection, I have read about it enough in this book already). I know, I have repeatedly emphasized building connections every step of the way because it's the core of marketing.

If you don't know the alphabet in English, you won't be able to write a sentence. Similarly, if you do not know the basics of marketing, you can't go beyond pitching. Forget about creating a sales funnel and customer retention.

In the next one or two decades, the concept of advertising is going to completely change from classified ads to human interaction. Let us start right now so that we can be a decade ahead of our counterparts.

One of the most important pre-launch book marketing is to design a beautiful cover. I talked to Derek Murphy, one of the best book designer and marketer of our time. Let's hear it from him.

1. **Hello Derek, You are one of the best known book cover designers today. Can you tell my readers some book cover design secrets so that they can sell more books?**

Go clean and simple. It's easy to screw a cover up with bad design if you don't know what you're doing. Especially for non-fiction, find a simple central image and add clean text (simple serif or sans serif). Clean and simple will win over busy and ugly, and you might get lost in the space between them. For fiction it's harder, but find an amazing photograph or two that can be blended together.

The text should look like part of the picture, not

stand out with bevel or drop shadow. Don't worry about being different or creative, try to look like a mix of all the bestselling covers in your category. It should "fit in" with those books so people can identify the genre and theme quickly. Colors can be used to indicate genre and get an immediate emotional response (red for thriller, blue/white for spiritual, green/yellow for finance, dark blue for business/professional, pink and purple for chick lit, etc.).

2. If you had no money at all, how would you promote your book? I am not asking, 'where' but 'how'?

Guest posting is the best way to promote books, with or without money. There are scores of high traffic sites that let you guest post for free – sometimes you have to apply for an account. Sometimes you need your own blog or writing samples to show, but not always. You can also just email blogs directly (blogs where your readers are likely to hang out) and pitch them an article. Bloggers need content. You're saving them work by giving it to them for free – but in return you can raise your visibility a lot. Jeff Goins started from nothing, just a few articles on his blog, then offered an email sign up for a short book "You Are a Writer," then drove tons of traffic through aggressive guest posting. He didn't spend any money but he nailed it and built a 100K list in under a year. Also nothing beats a KDP Select or free book promo, as long as it's done well.

3. **Let's say you had $500 to invest in book marketing. Apart from spending it on a good cover, where would you invest that money to promote your book?**

Advertising in BookBub or similar sites.

- http://ereadernewstoday.com
- http://fkbooksandtips.com
- http://www.ebookbooster.com

But make sure you have at least 5 reviews first. Also spend $100 on targeted Facebook ads during launch to hit #1 in all your categories for a few days.

4. **Most authors mightn't have the money to spend $500+ on Book Covers. Most authors hire a freelancer to design book covers for less than $50. If you have to give them some expert design advice, what would that be?**

Hire someone on Fiverr – but give them a clear indication of what you want (choose a stock photo image, pick a font from another cover in your genre and tell them what to make). When looking at Amazon, don't assume the bestselling books have nice design – indie published books might succeed despite bad design. Generally speaking, traditionally published books are better designed so use them as models. You can also try out my free cover tool on www.diybookcovers.com, it's got a bunch of built in fonts and is easy to add text and effects.

5. One of your books, *Book marketing is Dead* caught my attention. Let me ask you a couple of questions based on that book.

- **What are the common mistakes that can kill book sales?**

Poor design is a killer. It's much more important than people think. It doesn't have to be expensive but make sure it's done right. Often authors who do their own designs will love what they make, and they won't pick up on subtle cues that nobody else likes it. Asking for feedback never works because everybody will be positive, even if it's ugly.

Also, you've GOT to have some reviews. Don't market and promote a book with no reviews, you're wasting your time. Do whatever you've got to do, beg everyone you know – in person – who has an Amazon account. Stress on the fact that it can be really short, 1 sentence, and doesn't have to be falsely positive or flattering. And that they can just skim your book, and don't have to read it in detail if they don't have time. Through a party and when people get to your house, feed them well and get them drunk, then make them login to Amazon with their accounts and leave you a review before they go home.

- **What do you mean by an author platform?**

Your collective online reach – it could be your website, social media profiles, guest posts or any online groups (LinkedIn, Facebook). Different places are used for different things though – and very few of them can be used for "book marketing" as people think about it. You should almost never promote your books, like "Please go buy my books! On sale!" Instead just offer a lot of great content. Interact. Give feedback. Help people. You have to get people to know you and like you, before you'll ever be able to influence their behavior. Your book and link to your book will be in your author bio if anybody wants to know and they'll find it because they are interested in who you are – because you're an awesome human being. Whereas, if you just shout at strangers everybody will ignore you.

- **Name any three low cost advertising strategies. How much budget are we** talking about?

Facebook ads – not very cost effective, but you can pay 50cents (usd) per click, so for $50 you could get 100 clicks and maybe sell 30 books. That's enough to hit #1 in most categories if you do it in one day.

ProjectWonderful – it's an ad network, like blog ads, but much cheaper. You may find some blogs that are crazy cheap to advertise, like 10 cents a day, though higher traffic ones may be $1 a day (still pretty good actually).

Find some mid-sized blogs that are reviewing books in your genre, or talk about your genre, or are vaguely related, and ask if you can buy a post on their sidebar for $50 a month. If they haven't considered advertising before, they might welcome the opportunity. Though, if they are already using Google Ads, you can set up a Google Ad campaign that *only shows up* on their site.

However, advertising like this is rarely worth as much as a good bit of viral content – for $50 you can get your book turned into a new Powerpoint and put it on SlideShare; if the SlideShare is done well you can turn it into an infographic easily, or Image Quotes (excerpts of your book laid out over nice picture, or just on a color background). Image Quotes are awesome for sharing on social media and will get much more interaction than your ads... plus they'll keep working for you. The problem with advertising is after the spending, you're left with nothing. So it might be better to build some assets. (For example, you could spend $50 on Fiverr optimizing your website – improving SEO, editing your sales copy or author bio – and that stuff will help more long term than regular advertising).

- **How much do you think is a good budget for an effective book launch?**

$200 is a good budget, but you could do OK with $50. And you can do it for free – it's just much faster and easier to spend the money. But the money, by itself, won't do much for you unless you've built everything well – it's got to be a funnel, so every sale you make builds your platform. Everybody who finds your book should sign up to your list, because you have a fantastic opt-in offer, or review your book, or share it, because it was so life-changing.

6. **How can indie authors compete with traditional publishers? How can they win this publishing war? Could you give us a sneak peak of your upcoming book, "Guerrilla Publishing"?**

You don't need to compete with traditional publishers – their publishing model is broken and they are bleeding money. The question is, how can traditional publishers compete with indie authors? You see this more and more; publishers are offering "competitions" and crowd-sourced selection methods, because they have no idea what's going to be popular, so they're letting readers decide and tell them which books to support. Traditional publishers are pricing their ebooks lower; and there's a whole bunch of new hybrid options – none very successful yet but pushing the publishing envelope. Sites that crowd fund book projects, or sites where designers, marketers and authors can make a team and split profits or new publishing sites with totally different rules. For example, I set up www.readipress.com, even though I don't have time to accept submissions yet, because I can offer authors everything a traditional publisher can already. It's a myth that traditional publishers can get you into libraries or bookstores more easily; they will probably be buying the space at first, but bookstores stock what will sell, and what sells is determined by readers, not publishers. If you want to show up in bookstores, you need a bestselling book.

1 in 1000 traditionally published authors get any kind of marketing help or support. Most get sub-

standard design, a small advance, and then wonder what the hell they are supposed to do. Almost all traditionally published books fail to make any money, or just barely cover costs. When we think of "Traditional Publishing" we are thinking of that 1 book – almost always literary fiction or popular non-fiction – that got a clever, hipster cover design, appeared on the Colbert Show, and is in the front of all the book stores. But those results are extremely unlikely for 99% of traditionally published authors. Instead, authors complain they have no control, they got no help, they never liked their cover design, there was no marketing campaign. Traditional Publishing is actually dangerous, because it's so slow, so authors will spend 2 years in rosy afterglow feeling good about "getting published" but assuming they don't need to do anything else, like build their platform or interact with fans. That's 2 years of wasted time. If you self-publish, you can publish in 2 months and spend the same 2 years figuring out how to build your platform. (I have a lot of traditionally published friends who have given up on the system and are now learning how to self-publish and grow their platform).

As for as "Guerilla Publishing" – it means you *don't* have *to* play by the rules of standard publishing. You shouldn't be trying to do it "their way." You shouldn't be playing their game at all. They are playing croquet, you are playing laser tag. Their game is slow and patient and refined, your game is fast and active and exciting. The only question is: which game is going to attract the most players? Whoever wins the publishing war just means, which model is going to be more successful – right now it's a messy tie, but I think it's clear that authors who build their own online platform and make real connections with thousands of followers are going to be the real winners, regardless of how they published.

7. **Last but not the least, if my readers want to get in touch with you where can they reach you? I would be glad if you can offer them some special discounts for your books.**

www.creativindie.com - most of my books are free if you sign up on my site, and I always notify my followers when they can download new books for free as well.

Chapter 8

Post-Launch Marketing

Once you have launched your book, your job is not done. It's just the beginning of book marketing.

The big question is, what should you do right after getting published?

We need reviews for social proof. The fans that we have built before the launch are going to give us the first few reviews.

Ask all your email subscribers to write a review

Don't be shy about asking your fans to write a review. Be honest and tell them that you need their support in order to sustain. If you were able to become friends with your subscribers before the launch, you can be confident that they will go above and beyond their means to help you.

When a person buys your book, there's no

obligation on his end to write a review. Most people will write a review only when they are unhappy with a book. They will invest their time to complain about the book.

When someone enjoys your book, they will be happy that the money that they have spent to buy your book was worth it. They tell themselves, "Ah! Alright, this book was worth the $2.99 I spent." After that, they will go about doing their respective work.

The point is, a reader has no obligation to write a review. He/she feels no obligation at all until and unless it's extraordinary. For my very first debut book, I haven't received a single negative review, not even a 3-star review. Out of 38 reviews, 34 are 5-stars and four of them are 4-star reviews. You might think I haven't sold that many copies, but that's not the case. I have sold thousands of copies. I have received emails where readers have praised my book, but they do not take the initiative to write a review. It's not their fault. It's human psychology. Readers do not feel an obligation to write a review after they have read the book, unless and until they are immensely pleased with you or they like you.

We as marketers have to take on the job of forcing them to review. Let me ask you one thing. Have you enjoyed reading this book so far? I am sure you have or else you wouldn't have come so far. Will you make the effort to post a review on Amazon? Probably not, and I completely understand. Most people are reading it on their Kindle device with no internet. When they are done with this book, they might want to post a review, but due to lack of an internet connection, they will drop the plan. After a while they will get busy with their life and will completely forget about writing a review. We are all busy folks.

If only Amazon could add a feature to their Kindle service where a reader can post a review in the offline mode, then when the Kindle device is connected to the internet anytime in the future, the review will get posted automatically. Just like cloud synchronization, just a thought.

Anyway, I always request that my readers write a review. You are an author like I am and I know you understand the pain of not getting enough reviews. Help me and I am sure you will build your good karma. Coming back to the topic, ask your email subscribers to post a review for your book.

Create a hook, such as, "I will send you my next book as a free review copy if you will write a review." Sometimes it works, but nothing works better than building a personal connection.

If you ask your mom, dad, spouse or your child

to write a review for your newly published book, will they deny you and state that they are too busy right now? Even your close friends will come forward to write a review. **Do you know why? Because you have a personal connection with these people. You need to build the same level of personal connection with your audience.**

Email Amazon's top 1000 reviewers to write a review

When you get a review from Amazon's top 1000 reviewer, it carries a lot of weight. There are around 30,000 active reviewers on Amazon and getting a review from one of the top 1000 definitely speaks a lot about your book.

It's social proof for readers looking to buy your book.

You cannot expect the top 1000 reviewers to find your book on their own, especially if it's a newly published book with not many sales. You need to contact these reviewers and request them to read and review your book.

Most of them have an email address on their Amazon profile. I have made the job easy for you. I have already sorted them out in an excel file. Go to my website, http://www.fireyourmentor.com/ and you will find the details on the "Top Hello Bar."

You need to remember something. They probably receive over a hundred requests every day. You cannot sound like just the other guy who was begging them to review his book. You need to stand out.

Your book will be unique in its own way. Try to pitch how your book is unique and why they should read your book. I am sure you can find your unique hook to integrate with your email.

Ask blogs for an interview

Bloggers receive a lot of requests for guest articles, but very few interview requests. Most authors are too busy to contact bloggers with interview requests. Oh wait, that's just my assumption. Maybe authors aren't that busy, but most of them do not take the initiative to contact bloggers personally for an interview, and even if they do take the initiative, I haven't seen many authors contact bloggers directly. I have previously built and sold two weight loss blogs for five figures. I haven't received a single interview request, but I used to receive at least three to five guest posting requests daily when I was running those blogs.

Take the initiative to contact bloggers with an interview request. You will be surprised to see that most of them will respond. I get more than a 60% response rate, as opposed to a 0.5% response rate when I just pitch to them about a guest article.

I have showed you a format previously. Here's another format you can use.

Hi XYZ,

I am an Indie author. I publish my books with Amazon. I have published six bestselling books so far. I would love to appear for an interview on your blog. I can talk about the evolving self-publishing industry, the rise of digital books and book marketing.

If you would like to learn more about me, please visit: http://Harsh.Im

Thank You!

Regards,
Harshajyoti Das

An email should be short and simple. It should be to the point. I recommend that you link back to your author page, where they can find all the details about you.

You need to avoid sending such emails from

your primary email ID. Instead, create an email like this: press@harsh.im

Host Giveaways of the print version on different blogs

If you have done your homework to build connections with blog owners, hosting giveaways with them is going to be very easy.

To begin with, start with the blogs where you have been interviewed. Ask them if they are willing to host a giveaway of your book.

Secondly, go to all the blogs where you comment regularly. Ask these bloggers if they are willing to help you promote your book.

Thirdly, use BuzzSumo and filter out blogs that host giveaway. Build a connection with these bloggers and then pitch them to host a giveaway.

Hosting giveaways can be a costly affair if you give away your print version. I recommend you to find ways to give away a digital version. I have been thinking about creating an Android app for my book. It should come out within a couple of months. I will then start sending them the app instead of a print version. An app has more value than a PDF. Moreover, people hate to read on their computers. A lot of people don't have a Kindle device or haven't installed the Kindle app on their tablet.

Use the Asian Sales Army technique

Asia has the largest market for cheap labor. You can hire a bunch of VA's for $2.00 per hour from the Philippines or India. They will be your own private army to promote your book.

Dedicate all the book marketing work you have in your schedule so that you can focus your time to read and write.

You can outsource:

1. Social media marketing
2. Answering emails
3. Blog commenting (they can sign as Assistant to Author of "xyz")
4. Cold-calling, cold-emailing, pitching about your book
5. Keeping track of all your upcoming interviews

The list can go on. Free yourself from marketing because you need the time to write. We as writers need to spend majority of our time writing.

Hiring a VA won't cost you much. If you are starting out on a limited budget of say $100.00

per month, you can dedicate two VA's who will work for $2.00 hour. Each VA can work for one hour every day, six days a week. It will cost you $49.00 per VA.

We have almost come to the end of this book. In the last chapter, we will summarize what we have learned and what my plans are for Volume 2 of "The Art of Book Marketing."

I talked to Sheila English about book promotion using Book Trailers. Here's her interview.

1. Hi Sheila, you are the official trademark holder of "Book Trailer". If an author wants to use a book trailer, do they have to pay you any royalty of any sort? Do you have some sort of licensing?

Although I do have to actively maintain the trademark, I do not require a royalty. I do, however, ask that people who use the trademark by selling book videos and calling them "book trailers" have a credit on their website or social media site that says "The term "book trailer" is trademarked to Sheila English of COS Productions and used with permission."

2. For all the authors who have no idea what a "book trailer" is, can you explains it to them? Is it similar to a movie trailer? How is it created? Are there texts and pictures or motion

pictures? What should it say about the book?

A book trailer is similar to a movie trailer in that it uses a visual means of conveying a synopsis without giving away the end. The best book trailers are 90 seconds or less and convey the conflict, internal and external, of the book without any spoilers.

3. Let's say I have designed my book trailer. Where can I promote it apart from Youtube?

Anywhere readers go that allow you to post video.

4. Ad space on Movie theatres, TV are an option. How much does it usually cost to run our book trailer in a theatre or on cable? Can you give us some figures?

It depends on so many variables. Will it be local TV? Regional? National? Is it a 15 second spot, 30 second spot or 60 second spot? When will it play and against what? How many times a day will it play? You could run a TV spot for as little as $500 and as must as $100,000+.

For movie theaters there are variables there too. What city will it play in? How many times per day? How long is the spot? It could play for as little as $300 and as much as $100,000+.

The real question about playing a video on TV or in movie theaters is whether or not you have someone technical creating it because the formatting must be exact or it gets rejected. The formatting is a science all on its own and the #1 reason most people can't just make their own video and put it on television. Money not-with-standing.

5. How can an author go about contacting these people to get his book trailer to a theatre or on cable? Whom should he contact? How can he contact? Via phone, email or in person?

Go online, look for the station or network you want to advertise with and give them a call. They want your money. They make it pretty easy to get in touch with them.

6. If you have $500 to invest on book marketing, where would you invest your money?

That's not the right question. Or at least it's an incomplete question. If this is the question people are asking they are most likely novices when it comes to book marketing. That may sound harsh, but it's also true and I see small press make that same mistake as well, not just authors.

There's a feeling of desperation when you want

big things and don't have the resources needed. It's better to have a plan that includes money, time, resources and time. Yes, time x 2, because if you only have $500 to invest and nothing else, you're likely to be out more money than what you make on a book.

<u>Here is the right formula and then I'll pose the question people should be asking.</u>

Immediate financial investment + long term financial investment + personal resources + extended resources + personal time + volunteer time divided by goals = book marketing campaign.

The question really should be- What is the goal or goals of this book and what am I willing to do to attain these goals, giving myself the best possible chance at success and realizing that even meeting my goals can't guarantee that success?

It's not an unfair question. I would even say that the question should be required before you embark on a writing career.

7. You have spoken in Book Expo America, Romance Writers of America, RT Booklovers Convention, International Thriller Writer's ThrillerFest, Women's Fiction Festival in Italy, NINC and many other prestigious events. How can an

author get speaking engagements? Should they wait for event organizers to contact them or should they reach out to event organizers themselves? If they should reach out, how can they do so? Where can they find prospects? How should they pitch?

Your work, professional behavior and attitude are the best advertising you have, but you really need to let organizations know you are willing to be a speaker, what topics you feel you are an expert at and what, if any, payment is required to secure your services.

8. What does your production company do and how can it help authors promote their books? How can my readers reach you in case they want to get in touch with you?

My company specializes in reader outreach through multimedia. We create book video, but we also do book video distribution to reader communities, book bloggers, librarians, genre-specific communities and media.

We also own Reader's Entertainment online magazine which gets a good deal of traffic each month and has many free opportunities for authors to promote themselves via blogging, press release submission, article writing and so forth.

I can always be reached via sclover@cosproductions.com.

Thanks a lot for having this interview. Last but not the least, if I might have missed anything please add below..

I think the #1 thing I would recommend to anyone investing any time or money into any marketing endeavor is to know what goals you have beyond just selling books. Be specific in what you hope to accomplish and set at least one or two goals that are clearly measurable.

Chapter 9

Let's Learn From 'The Guy' Himself

Can you imagine earning $60,000 per month in book royalties? Don't freak out. It's not impossible. There are people who have achieved it. It's a possibility and we can make it a reality.

I have invited Steve Scott who has made it there. Let's hear it in his own words what it takes to be a success.

1. If you could go back in time and speak to yourself shortly before publishing your first book, what would you tell yourself to do differently?

Honestly, I would have focused more on the presentation of the content. While I knew my subject matter fairly well, I didn't initially hire an editor to proofread each book. As a result, many of my early titles had small grammatical mistakes which hurt their overall quality.

I'm now at the point where I work with two editors and a proofreader. I'm willing to pay the extra cost because I know they catch 99.99% of my stupid mistakes

2. What is the biggest mistake you have made on your self-publishing journey?

It relates to the previous question – not treating my books like a business. My overall philosophy is to write each book like a <u>very</u> detailed blog post that drills down in a specific topic. The mistake was to have the "blogger's mindset" where I could publish every thought and think it would sell.

<u>Since then, I've learned the value of a few strategies:</u>

- Hire editors and cover designers to create a polished look to each book

- Invest in tools, advertisements and products that will help me sell more copies

- Identify what actually works with my business, then spend the bulk of my time on these strategies

- Connect with other authorpreneurs and form strategic alliances where we help one another out.

- Experiment with new promotional strategies and platforms

I feel the self-publishing space is going to evolve and become more competitive. The only way to stand out is to think long-term and lay the groundwork for a business that will stand the test of time.

3. How do you manage to get so many reviews? Any tips?

I don't have a complicated strategy for getting reviews. I really only do these things:

- Launch a book to my email list, ask for reviews.

- Include a review request (with a link) in the back of book.

- Ask for reviews whenever someone emails me about a specific book.

- Build a "street team" of potential reviewers from people who are interested—contact them whenever I have a new book.

While reviews are important, I don't like to spend my day "refreshing" my author page to see what readers are saying. Instead, I focus on the fundamentals that get me the most amount of reviews, without wasting too much time.

4. Choose one: Slideshare or Youtube? Why?

While YouTube has a larger audience, I prefer SlideShare because it's a strategy where I can outsource 95 percent of the work.

4. If an author had just $1000 to invest in book marketing, where should he invest?

I'll give a plan that's worked for me:

- Sign up for Aweber to get an email marketing management program (@$20 per month)

- Sign up for the "Standard Monthly" option of Lead Pages. This will give you a high-converting squeeze page for capturing emails from book and blog readers. (@$37 per month.)

- Create a simple WordPress blog and host it through a reliable service (i.e. Host Gator, Bluehost.) Find a WordPress theme that's simple in layout and design (I like the options from Woo Themes.) Hire a designer to create a simple logo for your site. (Total cost: @$200 to $300.)

Start blogging (in addition to writing books to build up an audience outside of Amazon.)

- Hire a quality editor to go over your book and make corrections (@$200 to $400.)

- Hire a professional graphic designer to create an attractive, eye-catching cover image (@$100 to $250.)

This amount comes out to around $1,000. That's enough to set the stage for a catalog of successful Kindle books. The trick here is to set aside a portion of your earnings, so you can reinvest in the quality of each future book.

5. If given a choice, would you spend your time building fans and followers on social media or getting reviews & blurbs from major publications? Why?

Without a doubt, I'd spend my time building fans and followers. These are the people who would read my books, so I'd much rather engage with them, instead of trying to win over some major publication.

6. Apart from social media and your email list, where do you promote your books?

Really, the only other place is on the podcasts of other entrepreneurs. I try to schedule at least two interviews per week, which focus on the Kindle publishing process. I find that even though there isn't a direct correlation to the "habits market," many listeners will hear the interview and then go check out my books.

7. How have you marketed "Habit Stacking" and "Master Evernote" differently than your other books? This might explain why they are so successful.

I feel the success of these books was due to "the fundamentals" that I've practiced over the last few years:

- **Build an email list --** Most of my initial buyers are email subscribers

- **Craft good hooks --** Each book should have a compelling title that promises a solution to a very specific problem.

- **Write great books --** The more you can do to provide a great reading experience, the more long-term success you'll experience.

- **Get a quality book cover --** People judge books by their cover, so make it something memorable

- **Publish consistently --** Be consistent. Some books will bomb, others will take off. Do your best to provide a great reading experience, but once a book is completed, get started on the next one.

Overall, when you set up a good system before launching a new book, then it's more likely to become a best-selling title.

DON'T FORGET YOUR FREE ABM WORKBOOK

My books are more interactive. The **_Art Of Book Marketing Workbook_** is a special bonus for my dear readers. It will help you to not just learn the facts but also implement them. Please use the workbook after finishing each chapter to revise what you have learned.

Go to : Book-Marketing.org

Until Next Time . . .

If you want to read some bonus material, go to http://www.harsh.im/previous-interviews/ and read my guest posts and interviews.

There are so many areas I have left to cover in the first volume, but I plan to publish the second volume of *The Art of Book Marketing*.

I don't know everything about book marketing. I am still learning. I will learn even more in the next six months. I can then share all my newly-earned knowledge with all of you.

There are areas that I want to cover but I need some more time to do my due research and experiment.

In the second volume of *The Art of Book Marketing*, I plan to talk about the following topics:

1. More online opportunities
2. Decoding radio interviews
3. Press releases and getting in newspapers
4. How to become an authority
5. Various offline marketing approaches
6. Getting your books to the general public in your neighborhood
7. Making a difference in the world with

your book
8. How to leverage word-of-mouth to promote books?

There will be a bunch of other ideas as well. I want to share my failures and also my successes.

The year 2014 was the very first year for me as an author. I have so much more to learn about book marketing. Let's wait until the middle of 2015. I should be able to come up with my second volume by then. Not to mention, I have been talking to a lot of famous book marketers and authors who couldn't appear for an interview in 2014 because they were too busy. I should be able to grab their interviews in 2015 for my next volume.

All of my readers will receive the second volume for **FREE**. You can sign up to receive a notification on the day of launch here: http://book-marketing.org

I have more good news for my readers. I am launching a Udemy course on Book Marketing. I am going to offer a FREE coupon to everyone on my list. Don't ignore this rare opportunity. Go and sign up to be in touch with me: http://book-marketing.org

A Note to My Readers

Review If You Want, I Won't Force You

As a fellow author, you know the importance of getting reviews. You can help me sell more books with your review. I have a dream to earn over a thousand reviews for at least one book. I am counting on this book.

Each and every review counts. I know I can count on you because you have also struggled to get reviews for your books. You know the importance of reviews more than anyone else.

After you have paid me and brought this book, you have absolutely no obligation to return a review. You have paid money and I offered you this book. I understand that this was a pure business transaction.

But, I am asking you as a friend to do me a favor. A favor is all I ask. If life gives me a chance to return that favor to you, I surely will. That's a promise.

Here's the direct link to leave a review: https://www.amazon.com/review/create-review?ie=UTF8&asin=B00NUKB1Y6#

Regards,

Harshajyoti Das

Contact Info:

- **Fan Email:** author@harsh.im
- **Interview/guestposting/Press requests:** press@harsh.im
- **Amazon Author Profile:** http://www.amazon.com/author/harshajyotidas
- **Twitter:** http://twitter.com/jr_sci
- **Facebook:** https://www.facebook.com/harshajyotidas.author
- **LinkedIn:** http://in.linkedin.com/pub/harshajyoti-das/17/28b/52
- **Google+:** https://plus.google.com/+HarshajyotiDas

Author Website: Harsh.Im

CEO at Munmi IT Solutions LLP: Munmi.org

Founder of: FireYourMentor.com

MAILING LIST: https://book-marketing.org

2014 by *Harshajyoti Das*

All rights reserved.

All Rights Reserved. No part of this publication may be reproduced in any form or by any means, including scanning, photocopying, or otherwise without prior written permission of the copyright holder.

Disclaimer and Terms of Use: The Author and Publisher has strived to be as accurate and complete as possible in the creation of this book, notwithstanding the fact that he does not warrant or represent at any time that the contents within are accurate due to the rapidly changing nature of the Internet. While all attempts have been made to verify information provided in this publication, the Author and Publisher assumes no responsibility for errors, omissions, or contrary interpretation of the subject matter herein. Any perceived slights of specific persons, peoples, or organizations are unintentional. In practical advice books, like anything else in life, there are no guarantees of results. Readers are cautioned to rely on their own judgment about their individual circumstances and act accordingly. This book is not intended for use as a source of legal, medical, business, accounting or financial advice. All readers are advised to seek services of competent professionals in the legal, medical, business, accounting, and finance fields.

First Published, 2014

www.ingramcontent.com/pod-product-compliance
Lightning Source LLC
Chambersburg PA
CBHW071759200526
45167CB00017B/467